THE B

BEVAN

THE BEST OF BEVAN

THE WORLD'S FINEST

ONE-DAY CRICKETER RECALLS

HIS MOST *MEMORABLE* MATCHES

MICHAEL BEVAN

ALLEN&UNWIN

Geoff Armstrong, who worked with Michael Bevan as co-author in the development of *The Best of Bevan*, is the author or co-author of a number of other books on cricket, including *Century of Summers* (1992), the centenary book of the Sheffield Shield, *The People's Game* (1994), a history of Australia in international one-day cricket, *Whiticisms* (1995), with Mike Whitney, *Hands & Heals* (2000), the autobiography of Ian Healy, and *ESPN's Legends of Cricket* (2002), a study of the game's 25 greatest players.

Armstrong has worked with Steve Waugh on each of Waugh's 10 best-selling books (1993–2002), and has been involved—as publisher, editor or researcher—in books with prominent cricket people such as David Boon, Merv Hughes, Michael Slater, Bob Simpson, Geoff Lawson and David Hookes.

Away from cricket, Armstrong edited the first-ever anthology of Australian rugby league, *The Greatest Game* (1991). He also wrote, with Peter Thompson, the definitive biography of *Phar Lap* (2000), and with Ian Heads, *Winning Attitudes*, an anaylsis of prominent Australian athletes produced especially for the Sydney Olympics.

First published in 2002

Allen & Unwin
83 Alexander Street
Crows Nest NSW 2065
Australia
Phone: (61 2) 8425 0100
Fax: (61 2) 9906 2218
Email: info@allenandunwin.com
Web: www.allenandunwin.com

National Library of Australia
Cataloguing-in-Publication entry:

Bevan, Michael.
  Best of Bevan : the world's finest one-day cricketer recalls
  his most memorable matches.

  ISBN 1 86508 933 8.

  1. Bevan, Michael. 2. Cricket players - Australia -
  Biography. 3. Cricket - Australia - Biography. I. Title.

796.35826092

Set in 11/15 pt RotisSerif by Bookhouse, Sydney
Printed by McPherson's Printing Group

10 9 8 7 6 5 4 3 2 1

To my wife Tracy and daughters Olivia and Amelia

THE MATCHES

ACKNOWLEDGMENTS

First, I must thank my team-mates for making my career to date very enjoyable. Without them, it would not have been possible. Thanks also to Allen & Unwin for coming up with the idea for this book and then turning it into a finished product, to Robert Joske and the team at Duet for organising and supporting the concept, and to Geoff Armstrong for the work and time he put into the project.

PREFACE

Since New Year's Day, 1996—the day I straight hit a four off the West Indies' Roger Harper to win a one-day international from the game's final delivery—I have been recognised as a guy who goes all right in limited-overs cricket. Eighteen months later, when my perceived weakness against the short ball saw me ushered out of Test cricket, I was tagged a one-day 'specialist'. Today, no matter what I do, how many runs I score, how I make them, where I make them or against whom I make them, I remain, apparently, strictly a one-day player, at least at the highest level.

This is a source of frustration for me, but I have come to accept that there is nothing I can do about it, short of scoring as many runs as I can whenever and wherever I play, in one-day and four-day cricket, and enjoying every minute of my career in cricket. The rewards are still fantastic, the life privileged, the experiences wide-ranging and exciting. Five or six years ago I would have stressed out at my 'misfortune', to my own detriment; now, I go with the flow, and I'm a better person for it.

Why this book? I was never interested in producing my autobiography, nor did I want to write an in-depth analysis about friends and rivals, because that would mean writing about the good and the bad, and while I don't mind being critical about myself, I'm not too keen to put on paper negative thoughts about other players (not that, if I did, I would put down too many; the pluses would far outweigh the downsides). I also knew that I am not the guy to write a Mike Whitney-style book featuring a collection of witty and downright hilarious anecdotes; that's not my style. Neither could I, Steve Waugh-like, produce a travelogue of experiences from off the beaten track, because it is not me to venture into places unknown or unseen. I'm a shy bloke, who likes to keep to himself away from the dressing room, and while I might take in my share of 'sights' while on tour, I rarely stop to think about what they all mean.

There were two things I was keen to put on paper. One, I wanted to describe how I see the 'mental' side of the game, to explain how I have been thinking when I play the game at the highest level, how my thought processes have evolved, and also how my weakness in this area led to my struggling when I played Test cricket between 1994 and 1998. Too many times I have been asked, 'How come you never succeeded in Test cricket?' The answers, I believe, are in this book. I also wanted to put a few related thoughts on paper as to why I think some of the finest players in the game are so successful.

And two, I wanted to explain how I approach the art of batting, especially in one-day cricket. Because to me there is an art to it, and it is an art that has been downgraded throughout the history of the limited-overs game. The way I see it, cricket is going through something of a transition at the moment. Test cricket is still regarded in the game's highest circles as the only thing that counts. Many commentators and most officials and players grew up on it. But soon the game will be run by a generation raised on the one-day game and only then will cricket's abbreviated format get the respect it deserves. I think the general public can see it and the old fellows can probably see it as well, but at present the older generation prefers to think, when observing a player in full flight but wearing 'coloured' clothing, 'He's only a one-day player', as if the skills are not as important, or their level as high, and the pressures not as tough or relentless. The skills are as high and the pressures just as ruthless, but in a different way.

As you will see, I believe the most important thing for a batsman in top-class cricket is to take the pressure off yourself. Make the other guy feel the stress. Don't let the pressure build—and have a clear objective of what you intend to do. Believe me, after what I've been through, in Test and one-day international cricket, I know a thing or two about the impact of pressure, what it can do for your mind-set, and how it can ruin your game.

I've chosen as my vehicle for achieving these dual aims a series of what I've called my 'most memorable matches'. They are not all one-day games, though the majority are; nor are they all international matches. It was never my intention to give you a blow-by-blow account of any game; rather, I have recalled some great performances and my own involvement, and then gone off on any one of a number of tangents, perhaps analysing my own approach, or that of a team-mate or an opponent. Perhaps I might have used a game to comment on a major issue or controversy that came out of the game, or to remember an entire one-day tournament or Test series. I haven't been so much concerned with recording history as with provoking some thought and remembering some good times. With each game, I've included the full scorecard, to satisfy those who want to know all the details.

I start with the first match in which I ever earned some significant media reviews, a Prime Minister's XI game against Pakistan at Canberra's Manuka Oval in early 1990, and go through to the VB Series game at the Melbourne Cricket Ground in early 2002, when I made a hundred and helped win a game that most people thought was lost. In between, there are stories of good days and bad, and strange days, too, as I take you not just to Manuka and Melbourne, but to all parts of the cricket world, including Sydney and South Africa, Grenada and the Gabba, Kuala Lumpur and Karachi, Dhaka and the desert, Lord's and Lahore, indoor and out. From these combined experiences, you will discover some of what I've been through, and how they have turned me into one of the more high-profile figures in one-day cricket.

Throughout, remember that I'm still working on myself, as a person and a player. This won't stop until I achieve all I want to achieve. I still think, for example, that I can further improve my mental approach.

There are still times when I find myself worrying about technique, not being positive enough, putting too much pressure on myself. As you'll read in the pages that follow, I certainly used to go up and down too much. It was frustration. Now I can recognise the signs and settle myself down. I'm much more at ease with myself and consequently I'm hitting the ball pretty well.

I can only do so much. Try to score as many runs as possible. In pressure situations, you have to play sensibly, take advantage of your preparation, keep your nerve, and back your skills. And be clever. Cricket, especially one-day cricket, is becoming very scientific and very different to how it once was. We are discovering new ways to play the game, improving with time and setting new standards. I still hope to make it back into the Australian Test team, though because the side is so powerful I know that will be difficult. There are still goals to be achieved in one-day cricket, starting with the 2003 World Cup.

I truly believe my best is yet to come.

Michael Bevan
August 2002

GAME 1

PRIME MINISTER'S XI V THE PAKISTANIS
MANUKA OVAL, CANBERRA
31 JANUARY 1990

I was looking at a photograph recently, one that Mum had rediscovered. There I was—all of 19 years old, with precious little top-level cricket or big-time life experience—standing between two of the highest profile people in Australia: the Prime Minister and the Cricket Captain. I had just been named player of the match for the Prime Minister's XI against Pakistan, and there I was with Bob Hawke and Allan Border, with my head down, as if I was very embarrassed to be there. In many ways I was; certainly nothing had prepared me for mixing with such celebrities. This was my first real experience of dealing with the 'big boys'.

The main reason I was picked for the game was that I was a local. Sure, it was my first Shield season, and I was going OK with South Australia (SA) and at the Australian Cricket Academy, but I doubt that I would have been selected if I hadn't been born in Canberra. I had made my Shield debut six weeks before, and made something of an impact with a first-up hundred for South Australia at the WACA, but even so, I'd hardly done enough to be out there mixing it with the likes of Border, Mark Waugh and a fiery young quick named Waqar Younis.

This was the only time I ever played under Allan Border's captaincy, and I had the chance to bat with him, during a fifth-wicket partnership of 23, of which he scored 14. When I came into the Australian Test team in 1994, I actually took his spot in the batting order, he having retired after the tour to South Africa earlier in that year. Back in January 1990 at Manuka, 'AB' was in a pretty light-hearted mood. The PM's XI game was something that he was required to do; not a chore, but not a Test match either, and he was asked to sign a lot of autographs—he even made an appearance at a local shopping centre the day before—and then voiced his displeasure when the Pakistanis decided to use the afternoon for batting practice rather than try to win the day. For most of the rest of us, the match was a rare chance to shine against an international side, but I can't recall putting any undue pressure on myself to impress people. I was more concerned with not missing anything, with taking it all in.

One bloke I strongly remember playing in that game was my South Australian team-mate Darren Lehmann, who at the time was being touted as the next big thing in Australian cricket. 'Boof' is only three months older than me, but when I came into the SA team I saw him as being miles ahead of me in terms of status in the game. He was having an unbelievable season with the bat, scoring plenty of runs at a run-rate previously unheard of in Sheffield Shield cricket, and he ended up being 12th man for that season's Test in Sydney. But seeing Darren up close, in the nets with the SA squad and then out in the middle, I began to realise that maybe I wasn't *too* far behind him; that perhaps I might be able to succeed at the highest level. Scoring some runs—for the PM and in the Shield—didn't necessarily give me that feeling, but comparing my ability to those around me did. This said, today—now that I'm older and wiser—I don't think comparing yourself to others is healthy for your self-esteem.

My memories of the PM's XI game are somewhat hazy, but a study of the newspaper cuttings reveals that, for the Canberra crowd, the big frustration of the day was that the 'Lion of Pakistan', the great Imran Khan, did not play. The disappointment, the *Canberra Times* reported, was alleviated to some degree by the fact that 'the ACT representative [as in me] was named man of the match'. I received that award after scoring 74 from 84 deliveries, including six fours, in our innings of 8–266.

'Mr Hawke was quick to praise the performance of Bevan with the bat,' wrote Geoff Thomson, the *Canberra Times* correspondent, 'but was not so forthcoming about his one over with the ball.

'"Both Allan Border and myself agree that you played very well and deserved the award," Mr Hawke said to Bevan. "But it would have been a very different story if we had to take your bowling into account."

'Given the ball for the last over, Bevan conceded nine runs . . .'

I'd forgotten about that over. In fact, everyone bar our wicketkeeper Tim Zoehrer had a bowl. I was the last, called on to send down the final six balls of the match. I just made it.

I guess there would have been a few people at Manuka that day who would have predicted that I'd go on to play Test cricket. After nervously struggling through that last over of the match, not many, I reckon, would have suggested I'd be picked in some Test matches as a bowler.

I'd been sports crazy since day one. It had been my life and I wanted it to remain so. It was the reason I did just about everything. I saw school as a place to play sport; I wasn't the world's worst student, but my focus was on sport. I lived for lunchtimes and after school, working through all the under-age teams in cricket, soccer, and track and field. I never had any inclination to choose anything other than sport for a living—it was just working out how I was going to do it. Then, at age 16, I had to make a choice as to which sport I wanted to concentrate on.

And I chose cricket. Not even a major injury that turned my cricket around soon after could put me off the game. In my youth I was a quick bowler, but a back ailment that reared up not long after I decided to dedicate myself to the game put a stop to that, made me concentrate on my batting. Today, I'm most definitely a spinner, to the point that I think my body would snap if I tried to bowl quick. I have bowled seam-up in first-class cricket, but only very, very rarely, not for a long time and never with any great result. Once I bowled first change for NSW after a frontline quick was injured, and my first Test wicket— Salim Malik, very cleanly bowled, for 143—was from a medium-paced delivery (four overs, 21 runs, one wicket). Back then, though, when the docs told me I couldn't bowl for a year, maybe more, I was shattered. But determined.

My back malady had nothing to do with stress fractures, or an inappropriate run-up or delivery; it was simply bad posture. It reached the stage where my back was arched up, so that every time I bowled, I put pressure on too many wrong places. The pain was considerable at times, to the point where I had to stop bowling until my back was successfully realigned. But when I finally received the green light to bowl again, I couldn't rediscover my rhythm. Two years earlier, that would have been a catastrophe, but in the meantime I'd learnt that I was actually a much better batsman than I was a bowler, so I was able to accept what fate had dealt me, no trouble at all. It's not always been that easy.

I first played senior cricket in 1985–86, when I was 15 years old, but it wasn't until the following year that I started scoring meaningful runs: 171 runs in second grade at 57.00, and a further 118 for once out when I was promoted into the firsts (including an 83 in a semi-final). That season, 1986–87, I was named in the Australian Under-17 squad and was the ACT Under-17 Player of the Year. Two seasons later I scored centuries against the New South Wales Second XI and the Colts team from the Western Australian Institute of Sport, and a fifty against the Victorian Second XI. That was the year I established a new aggregate run record at the Australian Under-19 Championships, making 449 runs. The Championships were held in Canberra, and I hit hundreds against NSW and Western Australia.

Being based in Canberra, I had little idea of just how good I might or might not be until I started scoring runs against those Second XIs and in the Under-19 Championships, and then was chosen, following that carnival, for the Australian Under-19 team. The ACT had never produced a Test cricketer, and the local competitions—though they seemed ultra-competitive to me—were hardly littered with household names. I had a vision that I could make it big in cricket, but while there were other young players who seemed to me to be as good as I was, these cricketers didn't share my dream. While no one stood up and told me that I couldn't make it to the top, I can't remember anyone encouraging my ambition or driving me to get as much out of my game as I could. That was the mentality I faced as a cricketer growing up in Canberra.

The officials responsible for nominating the players to go to the Australian Cricket Academy in Adelaide were also the selectors of the Under-19 team, which must have helped when they were deciding who should receive an invitation to go to Adelaide. From the Australian Cricket Academy, I was selected in the SA team, largely on the back of some good scores in Adelaide grade cricket and for the Academy, and also—most significantly as far as my career went—for Mr Hawke's XI. The runs I scored for the PM's team definitely helped me. I was on my way.

PRIME MINISTER'S XI V THE PAKISTANIS, 1989–90
MANUKA OVAL, CANBERRA
31 JANUARY 1990 (50-OVERS MATCH)
TOSS: PRIME MINISTER'S XI

Prime Minister's XI innings

J Cox lbw Nadeem Ghauri	66
MRJ Veletta c Saeed Anwar b Nadeem Ghauri	50
ME Waugh c Saeed Anwar b Tauseef Ahmed	4
DS Lehmann run out	4
MG Bevan c Tauseef Ahmed b Aaqib Javed	74
*AR Border c Ijaz Ahmed b Mushtaq Ahmed	14
+TJ Zoehrer c Tauseef Ahmed b Mushtaq Ahmed	6
SC Storey b Shoaib Mohammad	19
JC Scuderi not out	8
DW Fleming not out	1
Extras (b 1, lb 8, w 9, nb 2)	20
Total (8 wickets, 50 overs)	266

DNB: WJ Holdsworth
Fall: 1-88 (Veletta), 2-104 (Waugh), 3-113 (Lehmann), 4-156 (Cox), 5-178 (Border), 6-187 (Zoehrer), 7-244 (Storey), 8-256 (Bevan)
Bowling: Waqar Younis 10-0-57-0, Aaqib Javed 9-0-45-1, Nadeem Ghauri 10-0-56-2, Tauseef Ahmed 10-0-47-1, Mushtaq Ahmed 10-0-46-2, Shoaib Mohammad 1-0-6-1

Pakistanis innings

Aamer Malik lbw Holdsworth	4
Shoaib Mohammad c Border b Waugh	33
*Ramiz Raja c Waugh b Scuderi	20
Ijaz Ahmed c Fleming b Waugh	15
Saeed Anwar run out	16
+Salim Yousuf not out	54
Mushtaq Ahmed c sub (M Wade) b Border	8
Tauseef Ahmed c Waugh b Storey	0
Waqar Younis not out	28
Extras (lb 2, w 4, nb 1)	7
Total (7 wickets, 50 overs)	185

DNB: Aaqib Javed, Nadeem Ghauri
Fall: 1-4 (Aamer Malik), 2-54 (Ramiz Raja), 3-78 (Ijaz Ahmed), 4-89 (Shoaib Mohammad), 5-97 (Saeed Anwar), 6-119 (Mushtaq Ahmed), 7-120 (Tauseef Ahmed)
Bowling: Holdsworth 5-0-28-1, Fleming 6-1-21-0, Scuderi 7-0-26-1, Waugh 5-0-13-2, Storey 10-1-25-1, Border 8-2-18-1, Veletta 3-0-12-0, Lehmann 3-0-19-0, Cox 2-0-12-0, Bevan 1-0-9-0

RESULT: PRIME MINISTER'S XI WON BY 81 RUNS
UMPIRES: G DAVIDSON AND LJ KING
MAN OF THE MATCH: MG BEVAN

GAME 2

SOUTH AUSTRALIA V WESTERN AUSTRALIA
WACA GROUND, PERTH
15–18 DECEMBER 1989

Throughout this book, the games I am focusing on are covered in chronological order. In this way, you will get a feel for the way my approach to the game has evolved, and how my mental thinking as I go out to bat—in one-day, and four- and five-day matches—has developed. The one exception to this rule in regards to order is here, as I now go back to a few weeks before the PM's XI game, to my Sheffield Shield debut for South Australia.

As I'd grown up in Canberra, not for one second did I think of myself as a New South Welshman. My dreams were about playing cricket for Australia, and I never stopped to imagine the experience of playing in the Sheffield Shield. Maybe if I had, I would have seen myself in a blue cap, but there was nothing about cricket in the ACT that said 'New South Wales'. I don't think the NSW selectors made regular visits to Canberra to check out the best we had to offer, and the NSW Second XI rarely featured anyone from the ACT.

Thus, when I went to play cricket in Adelaide at the Cricket Academy, I didn't have any compunction about representing South Australia in the Sheffield Shield. If anything, the most peculiar thing was having to sign a contract that forced me to return to my home state when my time at the Academy was over—because that clause said I had to return to NSW, not the ACT. I was too overawed to question anything—and a trifling thing like that wasn't going to stop me autographing the contract anyway—but I did think it was strange. As far as most cricket officials—within and beyond NSW—were concerned, Canberra was a country town. I was from the bush, just like, for example, Michael Slater (from Wagga Wagga) and Adam Gilchrist (from Lismore).

As it turned out, a number of guys in my year at the Academy went on to significant careers in big-time cricket, though not all for Australia. Within four years, Michael Slater and Brendon Julian were part of a full-scale Ashes tour, in which they faced Martin McCague, a fellow Academy graduate. Later, Craig White followed McCague into the England Test team. Others in our year who went on to first-class careers included Phil Alley, Dene Hills and Chris Mack.

I remember a match the Academy team played against the South Australian side, a one-day game that represented the first time I'd played against first-class cricketers. Naturally, as young blokes who'd spent a fair bit of time impressing each other in the nets and against various junior teams, we thought we were pretty good. And for a while that facade continued intact, especially when Dene Hills, who went on to score plenty of runs for Tasmania, successfully charged SA's then No. 1 paceman, Peter Gladigau, and put him over the fence. But Gladigau followed up with three very sharp, very accurate bouncers to remind us all that *he* was the first-class cricketer. When they batted, Paul Nobes smashed Martin McCague onto the road outside the Adelaide Oval No. 2, an awesome shot. These snippets gave me a glimpse of how good these top-class blokes were.

My year at the Academy was one of the best of my life. I shared my time with 15 guys who really enjoyed each other's company. It was as if I was living with 15 brothers; we lived out of each other's pockets, shared ambitions and learnt a heap about cricket. And I think we all matured as people as well. There was an excellent support network in place, but we were still living away from home—which I for one had never done for an extended period—so we had to learn to fend for ourselves.

A number of Academy players appeared in the Sheffield Shield during the season, and I was one of them. My debut came at the WACA, when I was a late call-up into the South Australian team after Peter Sleep was picked for Australia as a leg spinner. 'Sounda' was a top-six batsman for South Australia, which is why I was chosen as his replacement. It all happened very, very quickly; one moment I was playing for the Academy at Melvista Oval in Perth against a Western Australian Colts team (and watching Michael Slater and Brendon Julian make big hundreds), the next I was rushing across town to link up with the Shield guys. My new skipper, David Hookes, had never met me— we didn't meet until after I'd settled in at the Burswood Casino.

One of my strongest memories is of walking into the foyer at the Casino, a flash five-star hotel, looking around and thinking, 'Yeah, this looks all right, this first-class cricket'. After checking in, I proceeded down to the pool where I saw two of my new team-mates—one of them, I remember, was Darren Lehmann—enjoying lunch by the pool bar and again I'm thinking, 'Wow, this is fantastic'.

Early on, however, the cricket wasn't fantastic, at least not for SA. WA kept batting until tea on the second day, to 3–565, after Geoff Marsh (who finished 355 not out) and Mike Veletta (150) put on a mere 431 runs for the first wicket, 283 of them on the first day. A number of people had told me all about the WACA, about the bouncy pitch and the breeze, the 'Fremantle Doctor', that blew in every afternoon, but I must admit it didn't look too bouncy to me. Then we went in and crashed to 5–63, losing five wickets in 13 overs for 17 runs in a spell that ran from late on day two to early on day three. Hookes and Lehmann made nought between them, as two outstanding left-arm swing bowlers, Peter Capes and Chris Matthews, were superb. I'll never forget Capes bowling to our captain, who kept playing and missing, playing and missing, and I kept asking, 'Is he (Hooksey) doing that deliberately?' I was next in and it struck me that if Darren Lehmann and David Hookes were getting beaten left, right and centre, then I was definitely going to struggle. Hookesy later described the spell he faced from Capes as being 'one of the finest short spells of fast bowling I've faced for years'.

First up, though, I was facing Chris Matthews. Now Matthews is a bowler remembered most for being so nervous on the three occasions he played for Australia that he lost his way completely, but he was an excellent operator who took a mountain of Shield wickets for WA and Tasmania. My first impression was that he was way too big to be able to bowl. He was more a man-mountain than a swing bowler, charging in from out near the sightscreen, and he was a bowler with a windmill kind of action who would send down a series of 'jaffas' intermixed with some inaccurate, even wild, stuff. For the first half hour, I was embarrassing, playing and missing repeatedly, and I distinctly remember Paul Nobes, now a team-mate, coming down the pitch more than once to say, 'Hang in there, it'll get easier'.

As it turned out, Nobesy went on to his maiden first-class ton, and we added 221 for the sixth wicket. After Boof Lehmann was dismissed at 11.35am on that day three, we lost only one more wicket before stumps, and ended the day at 6–327, with Joe Scuderi on 26 and me on 106. I'd reached my hundred in 254 minutes, but then scored only six more runs—one four and two singles—in the final 73 minutes of the day. Having made a century, I was pretty obsessed with continuing to bat for absolutely as long as I could.

I had initially gone out there wanting to succeed, but realistically hoping for little more than to discover how I could go at first-class cricket. I ended up going all right, but it was a bit of an eye-opener. It was a huge jump in class, from playing in Adelaide district cricket on flat wickets to confronting a quality pace attack at the WACA.

I was dismissed fairly early the following morning, for 114, and South Australia did have to follow on, but we ended up drawing the match reasonably comfortably, with Darren Lehmann adding a dynamic postscript on the final afternoon by smashing 48 from 31 balls in a situation where most blokes would have been desperately defending to ensure the draw. After Boof was dismissed, with the game safe, I managed to get myself out for 2 (to Geoff Marsh's 'off-spin' of all things, his first first-class wicket), but I was still very pleased with my debut. From there, I kept my place for the next three matches. I was 12th man for the return game against WA and then opened the batting for our last three games, when I had the chance to measure my progress against some of the country's better fast bowlers, including Geoff Lawson, Mike Whitney and Craig McDermott.

I liked Adelaide, had scored a few first-class runs, made the Shield team, and enjoyed playing under the captaincy of David Hookes. At season's end, I was keen to stay, but then someone reminded me about that clause in the contract I'd signed when I first arrived at the Academy. I had to go 'home'. And then I looked at the strength of the NSW batting order, which included four internationals in the top seven— Mark Taylor, Steve Waugh, Mark Waugh and Greg Matthews—and three seasoned pros in Steve Small, Trevor Bayliss and Mark O'Neill. The Blues were the Shield champions, having slaughtered Queensland in the final. I could not help thinking that, having forced my way into one first-class side, now I'd have to go back to scratch and do it all over again.

SOUTH AUSTRALIA V WESTERN AUSTRALIA, SHEFFIELD SHIELD, 1989–90
WACA GROUND, PERTH
15–18 DECEMBER 1989
TOSS: SOUTH AUSTRALIA

Western Australia first innings

MRJ Veletta c Bishop b Hookes	150
GR Marsh not out	355
CD Matthews b Hookes	2
DJ Ramshaw c Berry b Gladigau	11
*GM Wood not out	26
Extras (b 1, lb 10, nb 10)	21
Total (3 wickets declared, 168 overs)	565

DNB: JA Brayshaw, WS Andrews, +TJ Zoehrer, KH MacLeay, PA Capes, AD Mullally
Fall: 1-431 (Veletta), 2-452 (Matthews), 3-489 (Ramshaw)
Bowling: Gladigau 42-10-126-1, Miller 28-6-100-0, Scuderi 31-9-103-0, May 38-9-126-0, Hookes 27-5-89-2, Bevan 2-0-10-0

South Australia first innings

GA Bishop lbw Matthews	22
AMJ Hilditch b Capes	20
+DS Berry lbw Matthews	0
PC Nobes c Wood b Matthews	124
*DW Hookes lbw Capes	0
DS Lehmann b Capes	0
MG Bevan c Zoehrer b Mullally	114
JC Scuderi c Zoehrer b Capes	38
TBA May c Ramshaw b Mullally	15
PW Gladigau c Brayshaw b Mullally	1
CR Miller not out	3
Extras (b 1, lb 4, nb 24)	29
Total (all out, 131.2 overs)	366

Fall: 1-46 (Bishop), 2-46 (Berry), 3-59 (Hilditch), 4-63 (Hookes), 5-63 (Lehmann), 6-284 (Nobes), 7-340 (Scuderi), 8-362 (Bevan), 9-363 (May), 10-366 (Gladigau)
Bowling: Capes 34-7-109-4, MacLeay 40-16-77-0, Matthews 18-3-62-3, Mullally 20.2-2-83-3, Brayshaw 8-4-8-0, Andrews 11-2-22-0

South Australia second innings

AMJ Hilditch not out	62
GA Bishop c & b MacLeay	27
PC Nobes b Matthews	59
DS Lehmann b Matthews	48
MG Bevan b Marsh	2
JC Scuderi not out	0
Extras (lb 5, nb 4)	9
Total (4 wickets, 67 overs)	207

Fall: 1-50 (Bishop), 2-129 (Nobes), 3-191 (Lehmann), 4-207 (Bevan)
Bowling: Matthews 16-4-42-2, MacLeay 15-3-40-1, Brayshaw 5-1-23-0, Capes 3-0-14-0, Mullally 12-5-31-0, Andrews 11-3-47-0, Zoehrer 3-1-4-0, Marsh 2-1-1-1

Close of play

Day 1: Western Australia 0-283 (Veletta 98*, Marsh 170*)
Day 2: South Australia 2-50 (Hilditch 20*, Nobes 2*)
Day 3: South Australia 6-327 (Bevan 106*, Scuderi 26*)

RESULT: MATCH DRAWN
UMPIRES: RJ EVANS AND PJ McCONNELL

GAME 3

NEW SOUTH WALES V TASMANIA
BELLERIVE OVAL, HOBART
14–17 MARCH 1991

It's become almost trendy to bag the Sheffield Shield/Pura Cup these days, to suggest that—because the Test guys are almost always unavailable due to their international commitments—standards have dropped and the production line has slowed. Inevitably, if the best cricketers aren't playing then the quality must go down, but I'm far from convinced that the current competition isn't able to produce great players any more.

Some Pura Cup cricket these days is ordinary, most of it isn't. I imagine it's always been this way. What the competition is still doing, as it has been since I made my debut, is developing a certain type of player, a bloke who is tough, confident, ambitious and resilient. The difference in cricketers produced by the Australian and English cricket systems is not so much in their skill as in attitude: English players can match us for natural talent but not performance—there is less emphasis on improving yourself and getting the most out of your ability in the English county set-up.

Every time someone says that there's no one coming through in Australian cricket, you'll immediately get a gifted young player such as Jason Gillespie or Brett Lee or Shane Watson or Nathan Hauritz coming through. As for the batting, it's always been strong—in the past decade, guys such as Michael Slater, Matthew Hayden, Damien Martyn, Justin Langer, Jimmy Maher, Matthew Elliott, Greg Blewett and Darren Lehmann have all played a lot of Shield cricket while also confirming that they're capable of scoring Test match runs if given the chance.

When I first played for NSW in the Sheffield Shield, I was—despite my performances for South Australia the previous season—only able to get a game when the Test players were away. When I did get my chance, I knew I had to take it straightaway, or else someone else would grab the opportunity. I did play throughout the FAI Insurance Cup one-day series that began the 1990–91 season—batting really well for 74 not out from 79 balls as NSW lost to Western Australia in the final at the WACA—but couldn't make the XII for the first Shield game of the summer, against Tasmania in Sydney. Going to training immediately after that final to discover I wasn't even in the XII gave me a real jolt, and shook my confidence. When Mark Taylor broke a finger, and Mark Waugh and Greg Matthews were selected for the Australia XI match against the touring Englishmen in Hobart, I came into the NSW side, and made 20 and 40, batting six, against Victoria at the Junction Oval in Melbourne. But back in Perth, where 12 months earlier I'd begun my first-class career with that hundred, I was relegated to 12th man and my main role was to take the drinks and change of gloves out to the Waugh brothers as they added a sensational unbeaten 464 in less than seven hours. On to Brisbane, without the Test guys, where I made 25 and 7. In the second dig, I was out after attempting a reverse sweep, hardly a sensible shot for a young bloke trying to cement a spot in the side. In hindsight, I didn't place enough value on my wicket, and I was probably trying to impress too much.

And then I made five hundreds in six innings, spread over six weeks. In fact, it was actually six hundreds—when I went back to grade cricket, in a week when NSW was not playing, I hit 164 not out for Campbelltown. To be honest, I couldn't believe that I was suddenly getting so many runs; it wasn't as if I had set out to prove a point, or to dominate bowlers. I simply found myself enjoying a glorious spell, where I felt supremely confident, where razor-sharp concentration came naturally. My strategy, if I had one, was hardly complex: I'd go out there, give myself half an hour to settle in and then attempt to blast whoever was bowling, whatever their reputation. In Adelaide, we faced Tim May, the best off-spinner in Australia at that time, and I smashed four fours off one over to reach my hundred. Against the spinners at the SCG, at a time when the track was always turning, I'd hit a delivery over mid-off and they'd put a fieldsman back on the fence, so I'd go over mid-on. Another fieldsman would go out to the long-on fence and I'd swing the next ball over midwicket. That avenue was then blocked, so I'd hit through or over the covers. At one point, against Western Australia, I swayed back and helped a Tom Moody bouncer over the keeper's head, like 'a shot out of a lacrosse game' one paper said. After that one, my batting partner, Mark O'Neill, came down the wicket and reminded me that I didn't have to reach my hundred by hitting the ball out of the ground. He could tell by the look on my face that that was what I was planning to do. I pushed my luck, something that was sure to backfire on me at some stage in the future, but for six golden weeks my confidence was sky high and everything I did worked for me.

I think at least part of this free-spirit attitude was a result of having played with the likes of David Hookes and Darren Lehmann in Adelaide. During my debut season, I'd seen these two blokes play shots I'd never seen before; now I was finding out for myself what could and couldn't be done at this level. And, in essence, I discovered that nearly anything was possible; later I'd learn that plenty can go wrong as well.

The last of my five hundreds came against Tasmania in Hobart, the end of a run that went 106 not out (v WA in Sydney), 20 and 104 (v SA in Adelaide), 153 not out (v Victoria in Sydney), 121 (v Queensland in Sydney) and 136 and 3 (v Tassie). The century at Bellerive against Tasmania was actually my most circumspect, including only eight fours and a six, but it was also in a sense my most critical, as we went into that game level, at the top of the Shield ladder, with Victoria, so a win and preferably an outright win was critical. Our plan was to score as many as we could at a reasonable speed after we were sent in, and we managed that by reaching 8–502 in less than four sessions. However, we couldn't then break down the locals, as they batted for nearly 12 hours for 550. With the Victorians' match against Queensland in Melbourne certain to yield an outright result—in the end, the Queenslanders collapsed for 79 chasing 193 (these were those now sadly no more days when they couldn't win the Shield)—we tried to set up an outright chance of our own by going for quick runs in our second dig, but time was against us and the match petered out to a draw.

Even though I scored all those runs, being part of that Blues team remained for me a tough school, a learning experience that definitely helped me. While the media were having a good time building up my potential—one Sydney journo managed to compare me, in one article, to Sir Garfield Sobers, Doug Walters, Rohan Kanhai and Sir Donald Bradman!—I never forgot that I was the junior member of a squad full of enormous talent and vast experience. I can recall numerous occasions when I was reprimanded for doing things I shouldn't have done. But I learnt a lot. Long-time Blues such as Geoff Lawson, Mike Whitney and Greg Matthews played it hard, a fact reinforced with much vigour by the coach, former Test keeper Steve Rixon, and this was something I took out of this period of my cricketing life. If it is worth playing, it is worth playing for all you're worth.

Off the field, as a young player new to NSW cricket, there was always a chance that I'd be initiated into the side by a practical joke of some kind. An inexperienced fast bowler by the name of Wayne 'Cracker' Holdsworth, who had been selected in the Blues side just before me, was also involved when they 'got' me. The prank occurred during a trip to Melbourne for a Sheffield Shield match when Cracker and I were told that two guys from the team would be required to speak at a major evening function . . . and, after speaking, we'd be required to sing a few bars of our favourite song.

At this stage of my career, my repertoire of yarns and stories was hardly overflowing, but fortunately Cracker—being the senior player— came to my rescue by volunteering to begin the talk, and I would just chime in when I felt comfortable. The hardest part was finding a song that we both knew the words to. And we did what most guys aged 20 and 21 would do—we delayed any rehearsals until the last day of the match (the night of the function), by which time I was a bit of a nervous wreck. I saw myself as a fairly full-on introvert and, considering I had hardly ever spoken more than a few words to most of my team-mates, speaking *and* singing in front of 600 people was hardly my idea of a great night out.

After practising Queen's 'We Are The Champions' with Wayne up the back of the dressing room one last time, I was putting on my jacket and straightening my tie when our captain Geoff Lawson casually mentioned that the function had been, in fact, two days ago and Mike Whitney had represented the team.

Needless to say, the boys—who had settled in for a couple of quiet post-match drinks—had a good laugh at our expense. But to tell you the truth, I was very relieved, to say the least. And a year later, when I finally did make my public speaking debut, I was able to confirm beyond doubt that it was not a natural thing for me to do.

In 1991, I didn't realise how lucky I was to be playing in such a great unit as that NSW side. Whit, 'Mo' Matthews, the Waugh twins and 'Tubby' Taylor all went away with the Australian touring team to the West Indies, but still we reached the Shield final, only to lose at the MCG. There was never a time when there wasn't someone performing; it was such a good team that there was always a team-mate who would put their hand up to do the job for us. I was quiet and shy, happy to sit back and take it all in, but you couldn't help but be inspired by the way everyone revved each other up, worked for each other. Cricketers feed off each other. If the stars have the right attitude, the young blokes who come in adopt that attitude. It wasn't until later, when I started playing county cricket in England in the mid-1990s, that I recognised the true value of playing with pride and confidence, being aggressive and giving your all. Until then, I thought that all came naturally.

NEW SOUTH WALES V TASMANIA, SHEFFIELD SHIELD, 1990–91 BELLERIVE OVAL, HOBART 14–17 MARCH 1991 TOSS: TASMANIA

New South Wales first innings

SM Small c Robertson b Bower	123
BE McNamara retired hurt	1
MD O'Neill c Holyman b McPhee	0
MG Bevan c Holyman b Buckingham	136
JD Kenny c Holyman b Bower	73
RJ Green c Buckingham b Oliver	15
+PA Emery b Bower	14
GF McLay c Holyman b McPhee	24
*GF Lawson not out	52
PJS Alley b Buckingham	27
Extras (b 1, lb 10, nb 26)	37
Total (8 wickets declared, 106.5 overs)	502

DNB: WJ Holdsworth
Fall: 1-12 (O'Neill), 2-247 (Small), 3-303 (Bevan), 4-356 (Green), 5-384 (Kenny), 6-397 (Emery), 7-433 (McLay), 8-502 (Alley)
Bowling: Bower 21-0-95-3, McPhee 29-5-135-2, Tucker 2-0-12-0, Robertson 16-0-54-0, Oliver 17-1-112-1, Buckingham 21.5-2-83-2

Tasmania first innings

RJ Bennett c Emery b Alley	76
J Cox c Emery b McLay	53
DJ Buckingham b Alley	56
*DM Wellham run out	8
RJ Tucker c Kenny b McNamara	165
BA Cruse c Alley b McLay	29
+JM Holyman c McLay b Holdsworth	8
GR Robertson b Holdsworth	99
PT McPhee c Kenny b McLay	5
SB Oliver c McNamara b Alley	8
TD Bower not out	0
Extras (b 5, lb 17, w 2, nb 19)	43
Total (all out, 186.3 overs)	550

Fall: 1-103 (Cox), 2-200 (Buckingham), 3-201 (Bennett), 4-234 (Wellham), 5-333 (Cruse), 6-351 (Holyman), 7-507 (Tucker), 8-523 (McPhee), 9-548 (Oliver), 10-550 (Robertson)
Bowling: Holdsworth 27.3-2-111-2, Lawson 27-6-81-0, Alley 38-10-86-3, McLay 43-10-109-3, Green 4-1-14-0, O'Neill 14-3-23-0, Bevan 21-5-66-0, McNamara 12-4-38-1

New South Wales second innings

SM Small c Bennett b McPhee	7
BE McNamara lbw Oliver	21
MD O'Neill c Holyman b McPhee	0
MG Bevan b Oliver	3
JD Kenny c sub (MG Farrell) b Oliver	31
RJ Green run out	59
+PA Emery b Robertson	53
GF McLay c Wellham b Buckingham	1
*GF Lawson not out	24
PJS Alley not out	1
Extras (b 9, lb 6, w 2, nb 6)	23
Total (8 wickets, 76 overs)	223

Fall: 1-11 (Small), 2-11 (O'Neill), 3-19 (Bevan), 4-42 (McNamara), 5-89 (Kenny), 6-162 (Green), 7-165 (McLay), 8-221 (Emery)
Bowling: McPhee 20-5-59-2, Oliver 25-4-76-3, Buckingham 16-2-39-1, Cox 2-0-8-0, Robertson 13-3-26-1

RESULT: MATCH DRAWN
UMPIRES: PT CLARK AND BT KNIGHT

GAME 4

AUSTRALIA V SRI LANKA
PEPSI AUSTRAL-ASIA CUP
SHARJAH
14 APRIL 1994

The Blues won the Sheffield Shield in 1992–93 and again in 1993–94, but the season I remember more is the latter one, because that summer proved to be one of the most significant in my career. With the international guys being away for just about the entire season, I now saw myself as a 'senior' player and that brought additional responsibility that I needed to handle. I thought I did it pretty well, and over the summer scored enough runs to win a place in the Australian team for the trip to Sharjah in April 1994.

I came into the Australian team as a replacement for Allan Border, who at the time had not yet retired from international cricket, even though it seemed likely that the just completed tour of South Africa would be his last. While AB returned to Australia to contemplate his future, Justin Langer and I joined up with the team in the United Arab Emirates, with 'Lang' in as a keeper-batsman because Ian Healy needed surgery on a bung ankle.

Just as it had been for my Shield debut, the first thing that struck me about international cricket was the lifestyle. It's a different way of life, playing for Australia, up a few more cogs from mere first-class cricket. I was now in the big league, staying at the flashest hotels, having porters insist on carrying my bags, having members of the public whispering, pointing at you, asking for your autograph. As I had on my Shield debut, I felt as if my first job was to do no more than try to take everything in and get an idea of how it works when you're playing for Australia.

The ground in Sharjah is located in the middle of the desert, a cricket oasis of sorts that was the brainchild of a wealthy Pakistani business-man who wanted to bring top-class cricket to the Middle East. For me, it was all a bit bizarre. On one level, I was over the moon at making the Australian team, but at the same time . . . you dream all your life of playing for Australia, and here I was making my debut in the Middle East. I wasn't quite following in the footsteps of Trumper and Bradman and Miller and the Chappells. No TV coverage back home, no chance of rain, nothing really at stake except for one small matter—I desperately wanted to take advantage of the opportunity given to me. That's how I approached my debut tour.

Making things a little tricky, while Lang and I were playing for our futures, was the fact that for the rest of the guys this was a tacked-on tour after a desperately long season. Actually, it was much more than a season for many of the guys, who had toured Sri Lanka in August–September 1992, then played a home series against the West Indies in 1992–93, then gone on a short tour of New Zealand, then an Ashes tour, then another home summer, then the tour of South Africa that involved three Tests and eight one-day internationals. And now Sharjah. And just to reduce the motivation a little more, while we were playing for pride, match payments and the prize-money, for the guys from the sub-continent there were extra incentives in the form of benefits that were awarded to particular players and then, I imagine, shared among the team.

My international debut was not one of the most notable ones, but through no fault of mine. I didn't bowl, didn't bat, but did take two catches as we thrashed an understrength Sri Lankan side by nine wickets. Second up, we beat New Zealand by seven wickets, and I made 39 not out from 63 balls as we successfully chased 208 with 13 balls to spare. In the semi-final, we made 9–244 from our 50 overs (Bevan c Jadeja b Kumble 25), which India passed in the 46th over. And that was that; my first tour as an Australian cricketer was over.

When one-day cricket was first played, the general philosophy seemed to be that you needed to score quick runs, and for most people that meant batting as you would in a five-day match and then slog a bit, when the required run rate became too high or you felt you'd scored your share of runs. I think it was Dean Jones who really blew that theory out of the water, who proved that you didn't have to take silly risks to score quickly. Remember the way Deano used to hustle back for two when he deflected the ball to third man and fine leg. I thought about the way guys like Dean Jones batted in limited-overs cricket. That seemed much more suited to my way of batting than outright hitting did.

I found that I could usually maintain my run rate by placing the balls into the gaps without taking risks. You can't score runs if you're out. A guy who hits out a lot, who takes risks, may pull off the occasional spectacular success, but unless he's a naturally pure hitter, like a Simon O'Donnell or an Ian Botham, he'll fail too often for mine. I knew that in any form of cricket, when you lose wickets the run-chase is disrupted, sometimes in a very major way. It always takes an over or two for a new batsman to settle in, which can give bowlers a chance to regroup or allow a new bowler to come on and get into a groove. I have always believed that if you lose your wicket, that can disrupt an innings more than your not scoring quickly enough for an over or two—provided you are still there at the end to help your team through. Slogging wasn't a necessity, but a clear strategy was. I told myself, just as I did in four-day games, that whenever I went out to bat in a one-dayer, I would try to be sure in my mind as to what I wanted to achieve and how I was going to achieve it.

The summers since have confirmed what I thought back then. Provided you have a game plan, I theorised, provided you know what you want to do and how you are going to do it, then almost any run-making task is possible. There is a place for risk-taking in one-day batting, I do concede—usually when the required run-rate has climbed above seven runs an over or in the first 15 overs if you are good at it—but it is not the only way and, in most instances, it is rarely the most effective way. Keeping the scoreboard clicking over means the bowlers can't get used to bowling at one batsman. Occasionally a brilliant piece of fielding can bring you undone, but so long as you don't try anything too silly, and work out the strong and weak fielders, the percentages are almost always in your favour.

Another thing I quickly learnt is that the reason batsmen in one-day cricket often take poor options is that the pressure of the run-chase provokes them into doing something that they probably don't need to do. When a batsman lobs a tame catch into the outfield, 'straight down the fieldsman's throat' as the commentators like to say, it's the pressure that has brought on this apparently dumb play. My theory is that you always need to do less than you think. And it seems to have worked for me.

AUSTRALIA V SRI LANKA, PEPSI AUSTRAL-ASIA CUP, 1993–94
CA STADIUM, SHARJAH
14 APRIL 1994 (50-OVERS MATCH)
TOSS: SRI LANKA

Sri Lanka innings
*RS Mahanama lbw Reiffel	10
MAR Samarasekera c Langer b SR Waugh	24
AP Gurusinha run out	1
ST Jayasuriya run out	8
HP Tillakaratne c Taylor b SR Waugh	64
RS Kalpage c Bevan b Warne	4
UDU Chandana c Bevan b Reiffel	18
+PB Dassanayake lbw Warne	7
CPH Ramanayake lbw Warne	2
AMN Munasinghe b Fleming	2
WPUJC Vaas not out	0
Extras (lb 10, w 1, nb 3)	14
Total (all out, 49.3 overs)	154

Fall: 1-30 (Mahanama), 2-38 (Samarasekera), 3-40 (Gurusinha), 4-61 (Jayasuriya), 5-91 (Kalpage), 6-124 (Chandana), 7-136 (Dassanayake), 8-142 (Ramanayake), 9-153 (Tillakaratne), 10-154 (Munasinghe)
Bowling: Reiffel 10-1-28-2, Fleming 9.3-1-27-1, SR Waugh 6-0-17-2, May 10-0-25-0, Warne 10-1-29-3, ME Waugh 4-0-18-0

Australia innings
*MA Taylor not out	68
MJ Slater b Vaas	15
ME Waugh not out	64
Extras (b 1, lb 7, w 3)	11
Total (1 wicket, 36.5 overs)	158

DNB: ML Hayden, MG Bevan, SR Waugh, +JL Langer, PR Reiffel, SK Warne, TBA May, DW Fleming
Fall: 1-25 (Slater)
Bowling: Ramanayake 8-1-15-0, Vaas 10-1-35-1, Munasinghe 6.5-0-28-0, Jayasuriya 4-0-22-0, Kalpage 5-0-29-0, Chandana 3-0-21-0

RESULT: AUSTRALIA WON BY NINE WICKETS
UMPIRES: K KANJEE (ZIM) AND KE LIEBENBERG (SA)
MAN OF THE MATCH: ME WAUGH

GAME 5

**AUSTRALIA V PAKISTAN
FIRST TEST
KARACHI
28 SEPTEMBER–2 OCTOBER 1994**

From the moment Allan Border formally announced his retirement, in May 1994, I began thinking about the Australian team's tour of Sri Lanka and Pakistan, scheduled to begin in the following August. I didn't consider myself a certain selection, but whichever way I looked at it, I realised I'd be unlucky to miss out, especially given that Dean Jones—who, like AB, was also in the team that toured South Africa—had also announced his retirement from international cricket.

Getting into the touring party, which I soon did, was one thing; making the starting XI for the first Test in Pakistan was another thing entirely. The team's batting order was pretty much locked in—Taylor, Slater, Boon, M. Waugh, position vacant, S. Waugh, Healy—and both Justin Langer and I had our sights set on that one vacancy at No. 5. Fortunately, I had a slight advantage, as I was preferred for the one-dayers in Sri Lanka that preceded the Test series in Pakistan, and did enough in those three games—averaging 55 over three digs—to be selected for the three-day game that came immediately before the first

Test. Scores of 38 run out and 62 not out in that lead-up encounter were enough to guarantee my place.

Those one-dayers in Sri Lanka were weird games. The series involved the home country, of course, plus India, Pakistan and ourselves. At the time, it must be remembered, Sri Lanka was hardly a world power in big-time cricket—their remarkable success in the 1996 World Cup was a little less than two years away—while both the Australians and the Pakistanis saw the games as a warm-up for the upcoming Test series. I guess in this sense, this made the matches a lot like the ones in Sharjah, where I needed to impress more than did my more established team-mates. Thus, we lost two of three matches in Sri Lanka, but then went on to win five of six one-day internationals in Pakistan, where we played in a tournament that also featured the home team and South Africa.

Our only victory in Sri Lanka was a strange one: a 28-run win over Pakistan that came about despite the fact that after we'd been sent in we batted terribly, making just 7–179 on a wicket that was pretty placid. I made 37 from 76 balls, one of those digs in which I could never find the middle of the bat. We knew we were up against it, especially when Pakistan reached 1–77, but they finished at 9–151. Later, this game was highlighted as one that might have been rigged, but I wouldn't have a clue about that. It was the same with another game in Hobart two-and-a-half years later, when 'Pakistan batted first on a seaming wicket and lost their top three for ducks, they included two spinners in conditions perfect for pace, and conceded 28 sundries when runs were like gold bars' (*Wisden*). Only trouble in Hobart was . . . Pakistan won the game! All out for 149, they then bowled us out for 120. I was top score with 24. I can imagine why this sort of game makes people think a bit—especially given some of the stories that have emerged in recent times—but all I know is that we were trying our hardest, but playing very badly on the day. Most likely, our opponents were as well.

My Test debut in Karachi, beginning on 28 September 1994, evolved into one of the greatest Test matches ever played. Mark Taylor marked his first Test as captain by making a pair, David Boon batted bravely and superbly for a second-innings century, Shane Warne was magnificent, but we lost by one wicket, after Pakistan's last partnership—Inzamam-ul-Haq and Mushtaq Ahmed—added an unconquered 57 on the final afternoon.

My contributions were innings of 82 and 0. The first innings, made after I came in at 3–75 to straightaway face Wasim Akram at his fastest, and then Waqar Younis and the leggie Mushtaq as well, was one of the better innings of my life. When I got out there, Wasim had the ball swinging 'Irish' in a way I had not encountered before (in the good old days, a ball would stop swinging once it lost its shine, but then some bowlers—reputedly Imran Khan was the first—discovered that if you roughed one side of the ball, and soaked it with sweat, you could make it swing again). Soon after, Mark Waugh was dismissed by Mushtaq and we were 4–95.

Steve Waugh was batting six. I remember when Steve came out, all he wanted to do was hit fours. He came down to me and said, 'I'm a bit too pumped up out here', which was a comment that helped me because it made me realise that it was all right to feel edgy. Not that I felt overly nervous; instead, I thought I was very calm. I guess I work a little differently from other people. I've seen players get really worked up about their first Test, but I just said to myself, 'Let's see what happens here, let's see how I go'. It worked well for me. We built a partnership, taking the score to 5–216, before Steve was out for 73 from just 85 balls.

After Steve was out, Ian Healy came in and we built another stand. As we edged towards 300, I started thinking, 'Gee, I could score a hundred here', and almost straight after I got myself out, caught at extra cover. I definitely lost focus; but, looking back, what is most frustrating about that is that I didn't learn: I did the same thing in each of the next two Tests as well, scoring 70 in the second Test and 91 in the third.

Maybe I didn't truly believe that I was good enough to score a Test century. I know that sounds a bit ridiculous—how could a bloke who can make 90 against one of the world's better bowling attacks not believe he could make a hundred?—but that was the way I was thinking, even though it might not have been apparent to those watching. In *The Age*, Greg Baum wrote of this innings: 'The mainstay was Bevan. He played Mushtaq without a false stroke, Waqar with aplomb and several times picked Akram from his legs through midwicket.' Still, my experiences at the batting crease in this series and since have led me to the conclusion that in your mind, subconsciously, you set yourself a level at which you think you are. And it can be extremely hard to climb above that level, hard to 'believe in yourself', if your gut feeling is that you're not quite good enough.

It wasn't as if I suffered from any sort of 'culture shock' when I entered the Australian team environment. The way the team prepared was nothing new, hardly dissimilar to what I knew with NSW, where coach Steve Rixon pushed us hard and well. Practice was tough, but that was the way I liked it. The off-field celebrity added a little extra pressure, but that was hardly annoying, and the fact we were touring a strange (for me) land mattered not at all. I can remember some senior players saying that Pakistan is not a good tour, because of the relatively poor standard of living and the change of culture, but I didn't care that there wasn't much to do, because I am usually quite happy sitting by myself, thinking things over. Some guys need constant entertainment or points of interest to keep them going, whereas I'm quite happy having a few hours by myself. There are not too many restaurants we can go to in Pakistan, not too many bars, not too many cinemas. What we did on that tour was build a cache of games and videos, which suited me fine. It was my first tour, and I enjoyed the experience.

My second-innings duck in the first Test came after Boonie and Mark Waugh were smashing them late on the third day. I was next in, but the way the guys were going it looked as if I might not even get another dig. Then, well into the last half hour, someone asked if I wanted a nightwatchman. I was a junior player in my first Test, so I just listened as a few of the guys tossed the idea around, all of them coming to the same conclusion that I wouldn't need one. Which was easy for them to say. Then Steve Waugh, due to bat after me, said flatly, 'I don't want one'. So I said, 'Yeah, I'm not going to have one', and straightaway, 'Junior' was bowled by the last ball of a Waqar over. We were 3–171. Out I went, the light suddenly much gloomier than it had been a few minutes earlier. Boonie hit a three off Wasim and then I was knocked over by a swinging yorker. Next ball, Steve was lbw. 'Heals' had to rush out without his thigh pad (he'd been packing his gear away when Junior was dismissed and had to get his pads and gloves on in a rush) to get struck immediately and painfully on the fleshy part of the upper leg, and we finished the day at 5–181. Ever since that day, I've always accepted the captain's offer of a nightwatchman.

Over the years, I've read stories of how animated and excited the big crowd became on the final day, as Inzamam and Mushtaq edged towards victory, but the truth is that there weren't too many people there at all. There was a heap of people at the one-dayers on that and later tours, but never a big crowd at the Tests. I felt throughout, mainly because we had Warney in our team, that we'd prevail, but the final two Pakistanis batted very well; it was more a case of their winning the game than our throwing it away. In fact, our best chance of victory came right at the end, when Heals missed a difficult stumping and the ball ran away for the four byes that won them the game.

Our great keeper was dejected in the dressing room afterwards; of course, we all were, but he was shattered, took it personally. It was an image that stayed with me for a while—it wasn't until I played some more cricket with him that I realised that he didn't always take defeats quite so abjectly. For me, even that losing experience was a lesson, as the guys showed me how they pulled together after the defeat. Players in many teams might have gone their own way, to console themselves, maybe to sulk. This Australian team accepted the fact that it doesn't matter how good you are, sometimes setbacks happen. We stuck together.

AUSTRALIA V PAKISTAN, FIRST TEST, 1994–95
NATIONAL STADIUM, KARACHI
28–30 SEPTEMBER, 1–2 OCTOBER 1994
TOSS: AUSTRALIA

Australia first innings

MJ Slater lbw Wasim Akram	36
*MA Taylor c & b Wasim Akram	0
DC Boon b Mushtaq Ahmed	19
ME Waugh c Zahid Fazal b Mushtaq Ahmed	20
MG Bevan c Aamer Sohail b Mushtaq Ahmed	82
SR Waugh b Waqar Younis	73
+IA Healy c Rashid Latif b Waqar Younis	57
SK Warne c Rashid Latif b Aamer Sohail	22
J Angel b Wasim Akram	5
TBA May not out	1
GD McGrath b Waqar Younis	0
Extras (b 2, lb 12, nb 8)	22
Total (all out, 88.2 overs)	337

Fall: 1-12 (Taylor), 2-41 (Boon), 3-75 (ME Waugh), 4-95 (Slater), 5-216 (SR Waugh), 6-281 (Bevan), 7-325 (Warne), 8-335 (Healy), 9-335 (Angel), 10-337 (McGrath)
Bowling: Wasim Akram 25-4-75-3, Waqar Younis 19.2-2-75-3, Mushtaq Ahmed 24-2-97-3, Akram Raza 14-1-50-0, Aamer Sohail 5-0-19-1, Salim Malik 1-0-7-0

Pakistan first innings

Saeed Anwar c ME Waugh b May	85
Aamer Sohail c Bevan b Warne	36
Zahid Fazal c Boon b May	27
*Salim Malik lbw Angel	26
Basit Ali c Bevan b McGrath	0
Inzamam-ul-Haq c Taylor b Warne	9
+Rashid Latif c Taylor b Warne	2
Wasim Akram c Healy b Angel	39
Akram Raza b McGrath	13
Waqar Younis c Healy b Angel	6
Mushtaq Ahmed not out	2
Extras (lb 7, nb 4)	11
Total (all out, 87.1 overs)	256

Fall: 1-90 (Aamer Sohail), 2-153 (Saeed Anwar), 3-154 (Zahid Fazal), 4-157 (Basit Ali), 5-175 (Inzamam-ul-Haq), 6-181 (Rashid Latif), 7-200 (Salim Malik), 8-234 (Akram Raza), 9-253 (Waqar Younis), 10-256 (Wasim Akram)
Bowling: McGrath 25-6-70-2, Angel 13.1-0-54-3, May 20-5-55-2, Warne 27-10-61-3, SR Waugh 2-0-9-0

Australia second innings

*MA Taylor c Rashid Latif b Waqar Younis	0
MJ Slater lbw Mushtaq Ahmed	23
DC Boon not out	114
ME Waugh b Waqar Younis	61
MG Bevan b Wasim Akram	0
SR Waugh lbw Wasim Akram	0
+IA Healy c Rashid Latif b Wasim Akram	8
SK Warne lbw Waqar Younis	0
J Angel c Rashid Latif b Wasim Akram	8
TBA May b Wasim Akram	1
GD McGrath b Waqar Younis	1
Extras (b 7, lb 4, nb 5)	16
Total (all out, 78 overs)	232

Fall: 1-1 (Taylor), 2-49 (Slater), 3-171 (ME Waugh), 4-174 (Bevan), 5-174 (SR Waugh), 6-213 (Healy), 7-218 (Warne), 8-227 (Angel), 9-229 (May), 10-232 (McGrath)
Bowling: Wasim Akram 22-3-63-5, Waqar Younis 18-2-69-4, Mushtaq Ahmed 21-3-51-1, Akram Raza 10-1-19-0, Aamer Sohail 7-0-19-0

Pakistan second innings

Saeed Anwar c & b Angel	77
Aamer Sohail run out	34
Zahid Fazal c Boon b Warne	3
*Salim Malik c Taylor b Angel	43
Akram Raza lbw Warne	2
Basit Ali lbw Warne	12
Wasim Akram c & b Warne	4
Inzamam-ul-Haq not out	58
+Rashid Latif lbw SR Waugh	35
Waqar Younis c Healy b Warne	7
Mushtaq Ahmed not out	20
Extras (b 4, lb 13, nb 3)	20
Total (9 wickets, 106.1 overs)	315

Fall: 1-45 (Aamer Sohail), 2-64 (Zahid Fazal), 3-148 (Salim Malik), 4-157 (Akram Raza), 5-174 (Saeed Anwar), 6-179 (Wasim Akram), 7-184 (Basit Ali), 8-236 (Rashid Latif), 9-258 (Waqar Younis)
Bowling: McGrath 6-2-18-0, Angel 28-10-92-2, SR Waugh 15-3-28-1, Warne 36.1-12-89-5, May 18-4-67-0, ME Waugh 3-1-4-0

Close of play
Day 1: Australia 7-325 (Healy 54*)
Day 2: Pakistan 7-209 (Wasim Akram 12*, Akram Raza 1*)
Day 3: Australia 5-181 (Boon 85*, Healy 3*)
Day 4: Pakistan 3-155 (Saeed Anwar 67*, Akram Raza 1*)

RESULT: PAKISTAN WON BY ONE WICKET
UMPIRES: HD BIRD (ENG) AND KHIZER HAYAT
MAN OF THE MATCH: SK WARNE

GAME 6

AUSTRALIA A V ENGLAND
BENSON & HEDGES WORLD SERIES
SYDNEY
12 JANUARY 1995

In the eyes of many observers, I returned to Australia after the Pakistan series as an established Test cricketer. However, while I felt assured that I'd be in the batting line-up for the first Ashes Test of the 1994–95 season, I knew I had a great deal to prove, was determined to do so, and the pressure that determination brought was, in the end, the primary thing that wrecked the season for me.

I put too much pressure on myself. In the press, I was being described as the next 'big thing' and, mentally at least, I wasn't ready for that, read too much into it, and attempted to bat as I perceived others expected me to bat. That is, perfectly. But I was hardly perfect, and after a couple of early failures doubts moved into my mind. I responded by going on the defensive—both in the way I batted and the way I responded to criticism—which meant that not only was I indecisive, but I never stopped to think why I wasn't comfortable at the batting crease any more. In my mind, things were going to turn around every 'next time' I went out to bat.

In the first Test I made 7 and 21. Making the impression I gave appear even worse, my first-innings effort came immediately after Michael Slater (176) and Mark Waugh (140) had added 182 for the third wicket. That demonstrated that there were few, if any, demons in the Gabba wicket. My limp performance suggested otherwise. In the second Test, in Melbourne, I scored 3 in 29 minutes in the first innings and 35 in 190 minutes in the second, hitting one four, and feeling as if I were in the dock on trial. Though we retained the Ashes in Sydney, after innings of 8 and 7, I was gone.

Mentally I was never convinced I was playing the right shot, that I had the right line, had correctly judged the length. I have found that in these situations, you tend to think that you're just starting to come good, and then you'll get one nick and you're out again. So you can convince yourself that it's just bad luck—that the main difference between good and bad form is that the bloke making runs keeps finding the gaps in the slip cordon whereas you keep getting caught—but the same thing keeps happening, to the point where you have to finally face up to the fact that something's wrong. It wasn't until I was dropped from the First XI that I was able to escape and play more naturally. And playing for Australia A in the World Series (this was the season in which the Australian Cricket Board included an Australia A combination in the World Series, to add interest to a competition that also featured England and Zimbabwe as well as the real Australian team), I found that I was able to do just that. More relaxed, I started making runs, including a hundred in a one-dayer against a similar English bowling attack to the one that had embarrassed me in the Tests.

What I didn't acknowledge at that time—and for quite a while afterwards—was that it was the pressure I put on myself during the Test matches that had stopped me playing naturally, and thus had brought me undone. Instead, I came to the conclusion that my playing naturally was a tap that I could turn on and off at will. I know now that had I gone straight back into the Test team after making that hundred for Australia A, I would have frozen again. I'm sure of it. But I didn't know that then. This was my first experience being an Australian player *in* Australia, and it was a real eye-opener. In Sri Lanka and Pakistan, I had never worried about what the papers were saying, or worried about whether the fans beyond the boundary were having a laugh at my expense or really aiming to hurt me with their heckling. I'd never had countless people I knew and didn't know telling me what I was doing right and wrong. I know now that I was not ready to play for Australia at that particular time. Maybe I should have realised then that I had certain negative thoughts in my mind, but I didn't. What should have been a learning experience for me wasn't that; rather, I listened to all the analysts who told me I had a weakness against the short ball, or played through the slips too much, was too defensive, too aggressive, too whatever. I should have gone away after that series and worked out what I needed to do to get back in. I didn't. Instead, I resolved that next time I'd play 'more naturally'. But it's not as simple as that. Not for me anyway.

The inclusion of Australia A in the World Series created a couple of conundrums, not least for the fans, who weren't sure which Australian team they were supposed to support, and also for some of the players who moved from one Australian team to the other during the season. Probably the most bizarre of these cases was Paul Reiffel, who bowled really well for Australia A throughout the competition and was rewarded by being 'promoted' to the 12th man's job for Australia in the finals. Of course, I went the other way—dropped from the Australian team back to Australia A—which meant that in the finals I played against the same team I'd been a part of for the first half of the competition.

The hundred I made for Australia A against England came from 102 balls, after I came in at 2–46. 'Suddenly, Bevan was a batsman again, as he drove and cut and glanced his way onwards,' wrote Peter Roebuck in the *Sydney Morning Herald* after I made that hundred. Greg Blewett also made a century, and two weeks later was batting in my place in the fourth Test of the Ashes series, scoring 102 not out on debut. He scored another hundred in the fifth Test, and then went on to play an important role in the Caribbean, as Australia beat the West Indies in a Test series for the first time in nearly 20 years. 'It was a brilliant partnership,' wrote Roebuck of our stand in Sydney. 'All summer, spectators have been yearning for confirmation that Australia's young players deserve their high reputation. At last it came, in bucketfuls.'

I know most guys say all the right things when they get left out—that they hope the fella who replaces them does well and the world's still a beautiful place—however, there is still an adjustment period where no matter what you say to yourself, you are still hurting. You're not dirty on your rival; indeed, I was genuinely happy that Blewey did really well. But, purely from my perspective, when he succeeded where I'd failed, it just underlined the question that kept nagging at me: why isn't it happening for me? I thought I was as good a bat as Greg Blewett—the hundred in the one-dayer against England confirmed that in my mind—but he was able to make Test match hundreds and I wasn't. I should have stopped to work out why that was so.

When I was left out, I had my first experience of how the Australian team reacts when one of its own is omitted. No matter what friendships have been made, for both parties—the guy omitted and the ones who remain in the team—the job continues, and so does life. I guess there's a fickleness about it, but what alternative is there? It's happened with much bigger names than mine; I've seen David Boon, Mark Taylor, Ian Healy, Mark and Steve Waugh all dropped from the one-day team and life still goes on. That's what Ricky Ponting was trying to say in South Africa in 2002, after Steve and Mark Waugh had been left out of the one-day squad, when he said that the twins had been 'almost forgotten'. He wasn't being narky or provocative, just stating a fact about life with the Australian cricket team. There might be a phone call, saying 'bad luck' (though it's not about luck), how much you wish the guy was still there and how much you hope he'll get back, but then it's on with the show. Really, it couldn't be any other way, for the sake of the new bloke in the team as well as the one left out. If you worry about how blokes outside the team environment are getting on, it's not going to help your own performance. Still, you need to understand this fact of cricket life, how the system works, and I didn't really get it until I was the one being dropped.

I've never met anyone who likes getting sacked. Some blokes might like getting away from the cauldron of top-level cricket, but no one enjoys being told that they're not good enough, which in one sense is what it means. I remember feeling as if my world had just disappeared and for a month I was very sour, very negative, a feeling that haunted me to some degree for the next couple of years. But although I got dirty, I didn't deal with it, which meant that when I got another chance, I'd replicate many of the errors I made the first time. I should have improved as a cricketer after I was sacked from the team, but I didn't. That didn't come until after I was dropped a second time, in 1997. What happened during that 1994–95 Test series—as I said I was having all these thoughts—was that I was putting pressure on myself and probably worrying about what people were thinking, and these were the real reasons I didn't have a good series.

The short ball! Early in that series I got out to a 'throat' ball from Darren Gough and played a few other short ones ordinarily as well. Immediately, I was reading and hearing through the media and elsewhere that I couldn't play the short ball, to the point that I thought, 'OK, I've got a problem with the short ball'.

I didn't really have a problem with the short ball at all—for the previous few years I'd coped with quick bowling pretty well, and in Pakistan I'd scored a few runs against Wasim Akram and Waqar Younis—but for the next three years I practised against the short ball, tried different things against the short ball, had heaps of short balls thrown at me, did hours with a bowling machine, was tagged as susceptible to the short ball, and focused on the wrong things. Sure, in 1994–95 I was struggling against the short ball, but that was because that was what the Poms decided to attack me with. I reckon that if they'd aimed at my legs, or concentrated on the 'corridor of uncertainty', that would have worked as well, because I wasn't mentally strong and that's why I was getting out. That's what I needed to fix—and then the short ball wouldn't have been a problem any more.

I've been asked whether the Australian team set-up let me down? Why didn't someone—the captain? the coach?—recognise what my problem was? My view is that, as they say, you can lead a horse to water, but you can't make it drink. It's got to come down to the player who's struggling—you can give him all the support in the world, but if he can't accept that he's got a problem, then nothing is going to change. I remember at the time I was busy telling everyone that I didn't have a problem with the short ball . . . and I still maintain that I didn't. But I wouldn't admit I had a problem at all. When Allan Border wrote a newspaper article in which he said I had flaws in my game, I stopped for a moment, but then thought, no, he's got it wrong too.

When I got that hundred in the Australia A game against England, I remember that I felt good about my cricket, as if I didn't have a care in the world. That was the first time I had felt that way all season. Personally, I found playing for Australia A *against Australia* to be awful, it felt terrible, but I made runs in those games too. As I said, the fact that I could score runs for Australia A against Test-class bowlers when I couldn't make a run for Australia in Tests highlights, for me, the fact that some of my problems were pressure-related.

AUSTRALIA A V ENGLAND, BENSON & HEDGES WORLD SERIES, 1994–95
SYDNEY CRICKET GROUND
12 JANUARY 1995 (50-OVERS MATCH)
TOSS: AUSTRALIA A

Australia A innings

ML Hayden c Gooch b DeFreitas	4
GS Blewett c Thorpe b Lewis	113
*DR Martyn c Thorpe b Lewis	13
MG Bevan c & b Udal	105
JL Langer c Gooch b Udal	16
RT Ponting not out	6
+PA Emery not out	0
Extras (lb 7)	7
Total (5 wickets, 50 overs)	264

DNB: MG Hughes, PR Reiffel, PE McIntyre, SP George
Fall: 1-11 (Hayden), 2-46 (Martyn), 3-207 (Blewett), 4-245 (Langer), 5-262 (Bevan)
Bowling: Fraser 10-1-36-0, DeFreitas 10-2-43-1, Lewis 6-0-48-2, Udal 10-0-56-2, Hick 8-0-40-0, Gooch 6-0-34-0

England innings

GA Gooch c Emery b Hughes	17
*MA Atherton c Emery b Reiffel	20
GA Hick b McIntyre	35
GP Thorpe c Reiffel b McIntyre	24
JP Crawley c Emery b George	37
MW Gatting lbw Hughes	15
+SJ Rhodes c George b McIntyre	23
CC Lewis not out	22
PAJ DeFreitas b Blewett	12
SD Udal lbw Reiffel	9
ARC Fraser not out	1
Extras (lb 13, w 7)	20
Total (9 wickets, 50 overs)	235

Fall: 1-40 (Atherton), 2-55 (Gooch), 3-100 (Hick), 4-105 (Thorpe), 5-143 (Gatting), 6-179 (Crawley), 7-187 (Rhodes), 8-215 (DeFreitas), 9-232 (Udal)
Bowling: Hughes 8-0-43-2, Reiffel 10-2-42-2, Blewett 8-0-44-1, George 10-1-33-1, McIntyre 10-0-45-3, Martyn 4-0-15-0

RESULT: AUSTRALIA A WON BY 29 RUNS
UMPIRES: DB HAIR AND TA PRUE
MAN OF THE MATCH: GS BLEWETT

GAME 7

YORKSHIRE V LANCASHIRE
NATWEST TROPHY QUARTER-FINAL
HEADINGLEY
1 AUGUST 1995

My first experience of English county cricket came with Yorkshire in 1995. The offer to play with them had come when I was touring Pakistan the previous year. I hadn't contemplated playing county cricket, but the offer was financially attractive and I couldn't see how it wouldn't help my cricket and life experience. I spoke to a couple of the guys who'd played county cricket—Steve Waugh (who'd played for Somerset) and Mark Waugh (Essex)—and they encouraged me to go, so I decided that I'd go over and give it a crack.

At the time, Yorkshire was still getting used to the idea of having an overseas player in its squad. It wasn't until 1992 that it first did so, and I was following in the footsteps of some high-profile players, such as Sachin Tendulkar and Richie Richardson. They hadn't won a county championship for such a long time, and were still in many ways 'old school' in terms of how they approached the game. And many of the supporters and administrators were pretty fickle, too, especially when I managed to score absolutely no runs in my first five County Championship matches. It was getting to the stage where my girlfriend

Tracy was being recognised at the ground and people were having a go at her about me.

After those first five games, I started to get back on track, but those few early weeks were a struggle. Just about everyone had told me that the wickets were low and slow, but in those early matches they were bouncy and quick, and I was thinking, 'The wickets over here aren't meant to do this'. And all the bowlers were really fit and raring to have a go. Rather than adjust, I subconsciously refused to accept the conditions I was playing in. Those same 'experts' who had told me about the low, slow wickets had also told me that county cricket was easy. But it wasn't, not for me, not for anyone, not early on anyway.

And then, as the season progressed the weather got better, the bowlers started carrying niggling little injuries, the wickets got flatter, energy levels dropped, the pace slowed—second gear was good enough— and I discovered the game those experts had told me about. In my first year, there were two sides to county cricket: it went from being very hard cricket to reasonably easy cricket. I finished the year with three hundreds in the county championship, and most people seemed satisfied with my efforts. *Wisden* reckoned I was the county's 'most successful overseas recruit yet', and for 1996 I was appointed vice-captain. However, it eventually turned a bit sour, as I became frustrated with the team's inability to climb to the next level.

This wasn't my first experience of cricket in England, because I'd played three seasons in the leagues. My first season, in Middlesbrough in the very north of England in 1991, remains just about the worst experience of my life and I vowed afterwards that I would never go back. I was over there as the professional, but I couldn't score a run. In return, I was heckled and harangued by the members. Even when I took a few wickets, they responded by reminding me that I wasn't getting paid to take wickets. Looking back, I never really recognised what I had to do to adjust to the wickets and the responsibility of being an 'overseas pro'. Also, I really didn't have any interests outside the game. Exacerbating my problems was the fact that there weren't any other Aussies around, so I had plenty of time to reflect on how miserable I was.

I said 'never again', but over the next few months I received a couple of offers to go over to Lancashire, and decided to give it another go. Only this time, I was determined to enjoy myself. I made sure I was going to a league where there were other Australians involved, with whom I could share the experience. I loved Manchester, had a terrific time and made a few runs as well.

I like the English, like them a lot, and I'm not saying that just because I married an Englishwoman. They really do possess an intriguing sense of humour; they can laugh at their weather, their class system, even—when they're going bad—at their cricketers. I like having a couple of pints and going for a curry after a match. And I like the way they are able to find a way to enjoy whatever circumstances they find themselves in.

An example of English humour occurred while I was playing for Yorkshire against Sussex at Eastbourne. All the lads came off the field that day to find someone had snipped the ends of five or six of the guys' suit socks. Needless to say, some of the players whose socks had been damaged were very dirty, but because, fortunately, my socks had been left alone, I was certainly able to see the funny side of it, even if it meant that I was now a prime suspect. I can assure you, I wasn't the perpetrator.

The identity of the 'Yorkshire Snipper' has never been revealed. I was speaking recently to a couple of members of the 2002 Yorkshire squad, Craig White and Darren Lehmann, and they told me that he had struck again. Considering there are only three players in the squad these days who were there back in 1995, I think it's fair to say that the mystery is close to being solved.

I met my wife while I was playing league cricket, in somewhat bizarre circumstances, which makes me think perhaps fate was lending a hand. On the same night, we both went to a nightclub that neither of us had been to before, and thinking back, I can't think for the life of me what made me go there. It was a long way from where I was staying, a long way in the other direction from where Tracy was living, and it wasn't a place that I would in all likelihood have gone to again. There were a lot of clubs a lot closer that I could have gone to, but I went to that one and I'm glad I did.

I must underline the fact that the three counties I have played for—Yorkshire (1995–96), Sussex (1999–2000) and Leicestershire (2002)—all looked after me really well and went out of their way to make sure I fitted in. Playing county cricket gave me an opportunity to play in different conditions, and the fact that I have played for three different counties has thrown up different challenges, made me assert myself in different ways, which has been good for me.

When I first went to Yorkshire in 1995, I had played in a very successful Australian team and a very successful New South Wales team—I'd only been part of winning teams. The first opportunity I had to see a first-class cricket team not working well was in Yorkshire. At the time, the players saw themselves as professionals, and there were a number of very talented players in the squad—most notably Darren Gough, who'd bowled a few short ones to me during the previous Ashes series—but in my view there wasn't a great deal of professionalism in the place, which was a result of the fact that up there, they had a very 'traditional' way of going about things. They liked to do things in certain ways and at that time nothing, not even the prospect of success, was going to change that.

One of the first things that hit me was the incredible amount of cricket they played, week in and week out, far more than I was used to playing in Australia. But I can remember one of the Yorkshire guys telling me that this was easy, that this was nothing compared to what it used to be like, how in the good old days they'd played 26 days out of 27 in one stretch. Which is ridiculous. It was no wonder that for too much of the time they played without intensity, with the foot off the accelerator.

The most disappointing aspect of my time in county cricket is that, so far, I haven't played for a team that has won anything. Yorkshire were closer than they realised—at the time they just didn't know how to win, weren't comfortable with the idea of taking the chances they needed to take if they were going to succeed. It seems they've reached that point now, to the extent that they dominated the 2001 county championship.

In 1995, my first year there, we did reach a semi-final of the NatWest Trophy and managed some encouraging performances in the championship (improving from 13th to 8th) and the Benson & Hedges Cup (quarter-finals). Our quarter-final victory over arch rivals Lancashire in the NatWest Trophy was one of the highlights of my time there. The thrilling 60-overs match—played, appropriately enough, on Yorkshire Day—went down to the final over, in front of a full house at Headingley. In fact, the game was more than a sell-out, with a conservatively estimated 18 900 people getting in, another 2000 locked out of the ground, unable to get a ticket, and many others perched on balconies and even rooftops of houses and flats adjacent to the ground. This was apparently the first time since the 1950s that the famous ground had been full for a game between two county sides, while the win meant Yorkshire went to the semi-finals of the competition for the first time in 13 years.

It was as raucous an atmosphere as you can imagine in English cricket—as vibrant as any one-day international, perhaps more so—and Goughie, a proud Yorkshireman who'd ignored a directive from the English selectors not to play because of a bruised foot, revelled in it early on, producing a fiery spell that saw our opponents collapse to 4–47. From there, they did well to battle to the 54th over and 169 all out. I think most of our supporters thought we'd do it easily, but there was plenty in the wicket and Lancashire had a fellow called Wasim Akram in their line-up. When we stumbled to 4–69, the game was on.

We had 60 overs to get the runs, and I decided to use them, taking 126 balls for my 60 not out that helped get us home. I can remember more than a few times when the louder members of the crowd wondered whether I was going too slowly, but I always felt that if I was there at the end, then that would be our best chance of getting the win. Ashley Metcalfe, a very handy batsman, played a key, aggressive knock, and

Goughie came out and hit a brief but important 10 that kept the run-rate active at a vital stage. When he was out at 8–155 it was still anyone's game, but I managed to hit Glen Chapple for 10 in three balls during the 58th over, which almost got us home.

At the start of the final over, bowled by Chapple, we needed three to win, and I had the strike. Ideally, as the senior batsman, I'd have liked to have taken responsibility for the last runs, but when a single presented itself off the first ball, I knew I had to take it. In this situation, you can leave yourself open to criticism if the last two wickets fall straightaway, but I will always believe that the odds are in your favour if you take every run available. And so it proved in this case. Peter Hartley couldn't get a run from Chapple's second delivery, but then pushed the third through midwicket for two, and victory was ours. Then it was a mad dash for the change room as the whole of Leeds (or so it seemed) poured onto the ground to celebrate.

Of my many knocks in county cricket, one of my most pleasurable came on 8 May 2002, my 32nd birthday, for Leicestershire against Warwickshire at my new home ground, Grace Road. I had been struggling to that point of the season, and felt out of nick, which I put down to the fact that I was batting on wickets I wasn't used to. On this day, the track was a slow seamer and after two hours I was no more than 20. If anyone at this point had told me county cricket was easy, I'd have given them a real rev up. Even when I got to 80 I was still battling, and I spent the final hour of the day in the 90s (99 not out at stumps), but I was proud of the fact that I persisted. It was good for me and, I hope, a productive example for my team-mates, who I knew were looking to their overseas import for some runs and self-belief. That the innings gave us a platform to go on and win the match (I finished with 146, made in 438 minutes, and we won by seven wickets), and then enjoy a run of good form that had us in second place on the championship ladder as late as mid-June, was extremely satisfying.

I'm not sure I could have played that sort of innings in my Yorkshire days. Back then, I would have stressed out about the fact I was struggling, would have been too keen to impress, would have been worried about the provocative things that were being said behind my back, or to my partner, about my poor form going into the game, about the way I was batting. Nowadays, I don't stop to worry if I fail a couple of times, because I've learnt that if I do the right things and don't let the expectations tighten up my game, then the runs will come and I will eventually deliver what is desired of me.

YORKSHIRE V LANCASHIRE, NATWEST TROPHY QUARTER-FINAL, 1995
HEADINGLEY, LEEDS
1 AUGUST 1995 (60-OVERS MATCH)
TOSS: LANCASHIRE

Lancashire innings

MA Atherton c Blakey b Gough	5
JER Gallian lbw Robinson	7
JP Crawley lbw White	13
NH Fairbrother st Blakey b Grayson	46
GD Lloyd c Blakey b White	0
*M Watkinson c White b Robinson	55
Wasim Akram c Byas b Bevan	0
+WK Hegg c Blakey b Hartley	7
ID Austin not out	15
G Yates run out	9
G Chapple lbw Robinson	0
Extras (lb 2, w 2, nb 8)	12
Total (all out, 53.3 overs)	169

Fall: 1-8, 2-14, 3-47, 4-47, 5-117, 6-118, 7-136, 8-149, 9-169, 10-169
Bowling: Gough 9-2-18-1, Hartley 12-0-50-1, Robinson 10.3-2-21-3, White 9-0-28-2, Grayson 9-0-36-1, Bevan 4-0-14-1

Yorkshire innings

SA Kellett c Hegg b Austin	6
MP Vaughan c Fairbrother b Austin	14
*D Byas c Hegg b Yates	31
MG Bevan not out	60
C White c Crawley b Watkinson	0
AA Metcalfe c Fairbrother b Watkinson	33
+RJ Blakey run out	1
AP Grayson c Hegg b Chapple	7
D Gough b Austin	10
PJ Hartley not out	3
Extras (w 3, nb 2)	5
Total (8 wickets, 59.3 overs)	170

DNB: MA Robinson
Fall: 1-20, 2-29, 3-66, 4-69, 5-121, 6-123, 7-132, 8-155
Bowling: Wasim Akram 12-1-38-0, Chapple 11.3-1-47-1, Austin 12-2-32-3, Watkinson 12-0-36-2, Yates 12-2-17-1

RESULT: YORKSHIRE WON BY TWO WICKETS
UMPIRES: B DUDLESTON AND DR SHEPHERD
MAN OF THE MATCH: MG BEVAN

GAME 8

AUSTRALIA V WEST INDIES
BENSON & HEDGES WORLD SERIES
SYDNEY
1 JANUARY 1996

In much the same way that I've found it hard to shake the tag about my reputed weakness against the short ball in Test cricket, I've found it difficult to stop people asking me about the game I helped win for Australia by hitting the final ball of the game for four. It seems this one night will always be my signature piece in cricket. It was a great moment in my life, and one of the best innings I've played, but because it came at a time when critics were questioning my credentials for the longer game, it instigated a push to have me tagged as purely a 'one-day' batsman—good enough for the limited-overs matches but not for the Tests. I've had to carry that label ever since.

This game is like my 'Tied Test'. Just as there are tens of thousands of people who claim they were at the Gabba in December 1960 to see the conclusion of arguably cricket's most exciting Test, I am constantly amazed by the number of people who tell me, always very early in the first conversation I ever have with them, that they were there that night. There must have been 80 000, maybe 100 000, people at the Sydney Cricket Ground that night! The truth is that it rained halfway through the match and for a while it seemed that the game might be abandoned. I reckon at least half the crowd went home.

At this stage the selectors weren't committed to the idea of having different players in the Test and one-day teams. Previously, it had only been truly special one-day players, such as Simon O'Donnell and Dean Jones, who had stayed in the one-day squad despite being left out of the Test XI, but for this 1995–96 season David Boon was dropped from the Australian team for the World Series competition, and Steve Waugh was injured, so Stuart Law and I came into the side. At the time, Stuey was definitely in front of me in the queue for a spot in the Test XI (he actually played in the Perth Test, and scored 54 not out in what proved to be his only Test innings), so had Tugga been fit for those one-dayers, I probably would have been the one to miss out.

I went into the game against the Windies in pretty good nick, having made 32 not out, 44 not out and 18 not out in our first three matches. I gained some confidence from these innings, especially the last, which came off 16 balls in a run-chase against Sri Lanka at the SCG in which we got home, pursuing 257, with two balls and five wickets to spare. Now, against the Windies, I found myself the last remaining specialist batsman at 6–38 in a chase for 173. Which was tricky, but not impossible, even though the pitch was juiced up after the rain. I always felt that I had handled myself well in this type of situation in the past, as the key player in a run-chase, and on this occasion, with Ian Healy, added 36 before Heals was bowled by off-spinner Roger Harper. Seven for 74.

Our task wasn't quite as awkward as it looked. One, the wicket had quietened down. Two, the Windies' two big guns—Courtney Walsh and Curtly Ambrose—had bowled most of their overs in an effort to knock us over completely, which left the inexperienced Otis Gibson plus medium-pacer Phil Simmons and Harper to bowl most of the remaining overs. Three, two of the blokes I had to bat with—Paul Reiffel and Shane Warne—were hardly duffers. And four, because we were only chasing 172 in a rain-shortened match, it wasn't as if we needed a huge amount of runs; in this sense it wasn't too different to being 7–170 chasing 270 at the 35-over mark in a 50-overs match.

Before I go out to bat in situations such as this, I get quite anxious, but as you go out to the middle you start to concentrate on what you are about to do and that feeling subsides. The trick is to keep your concentration, not to let your nerves overtake your focus. Unlike the previous season's Test matches, I was able to do this. If I'm on edge in a thrilling finish, but calm and in control, then I know we have a chance. It's actually a quite glorious feeling, especially if you sense that your opponents aren't as relaxed as you are.

One of the keys in a run-chase is that you don't want to run your race too early, if for no other reason than that the further you get into the innings, the more pressure is placed on the bowlers and the fieldsmen. It's not just the batsmen who are under pressure. Bowlers who look composed and excellent in overs 30 to 40 can suddenly lose their line, length and skill in the final five to 10 overs. It happens time and again. But that said, you can't simply defend until the task gets too demanding. You have to do the sums, and work within the framework in which you perform at your best. I've never had a problem with leaving it to the last moment. Whether that's right or wrong for everyone, I don't know, but it is the way I operate; I make sure that I do my job, which is to try to win games as a middle-order batsman. Of course, there have been times when this strategy hasn't worked out, and when that happens I always reassure myself by stressing that this is the approach that is most likely to work for me, and for the team. In one-day international cricket, you've got to be prepared to lose some as well.

I have no doubt that, whatever the wickets situation, you can work comfortably in a pursuit in which the required run-rate is five or six runs an over. Once you get beyond seven an over, it can get awkward, and the risks you need to take can be too hazardous. This was one of the key factors of the game against the Windies; while we were seven wickets down, the runs per over needed were never too demanding.

And just as crucially, if the required run-rate is around six an over, just as the batsmen can't afford to let it get too much harder, the bowlers can't afford to give anything away. What this means is that, especially during the overs from around 30 to 45, the fielding captain is loathe to experiment. He sets conventional fields, usually five on the boundary, four within the fielding circles. And in doing so, that skipper is showing his bowler's hand. If fine leg comes up, the bowler is hardly likely to attack leg stump; if there's a man deep at cover, but deep midwicket is open, you can bet the bowler's line will be on or outside off-stump. This isn't rocket science, sure, but it does mean that, as the senior batsman, you can plan your counterattack.

In these situations, I believe that you've just got to keep telling yourself that you'll be there at the end. Give yourself an opportunity to win the match. 'Even if we don't win, we can get close.' That's all I recall saying to myself, constantly, until the last couple of overs. 'Pistol' Reiffel batted really well, to the point that just before he was dismissed, we firmly believed we were going to win. He scored 34 from 48 balls, and when he was caught by Carl Hooper off Simmons, we only needed 16 to win, from a maximum 10 deliveries.

In the last few overs, one strategy stayed strong in my mind: I knew Roger Harper was going to bowl again and I thought it might be prudent to wait for him. However, I had to keep waiting and waiting, not realising that stand-in Windies captain Courtney Walsh's plan was to keep Harper only for the death. So I had to be patient, not play any rash shots, wait for that moment.

Still, when I hit the last ball of Phil Simmons' fifth over, the 49th, to the midwicket fence, the equation was seven to win from six deliveries, to be bowled by Harper. A single from the first ball, and then a mix-up, mostly my fault, and Warney was run out. Six to win from four.

When Glenn McGrath strode out for the final four deliveries, he looked ultra-serious, jaws clenched tight . . . until he reached the wicket, when he looked up at me and smiled, which broke the tension a little. My main concern was mapping out in my mind exactly what I wanted to do, but then it didn't work out the way I wanted. Harper actually bowled a superb final over: we got two singles and needed four from two, and then four from one when he bowled a really good dot ball, straight at the blockhole, which I couldn't do anything with. So it was all down to the last delivery . . .

Twelve months earlier, when I batted in the Ashes Tests, my mind was filled with 'what ifs'. Here, despite the pressure of a make-or-break situation, for me there was no thought as to what would happen if we didn't get the runs or what would happen if we did. I was focused on what I had to do to give myself the best chance to hit the boundary we needed. I went through all the possibilities, all the shots I thought I could play, the types of delivery Harper would most likely bowl . . .

I quickly narrowed my options down to three. There were three significant gaps in the outfield: I could go over midwicket, over cover or hit straight. But I was sure he was going to spear in a faster one, and when he did I was ready . . .

Hit it straight.

By stepping away to the legside I gave myself a little room. Maybe he fired it in a fraction shorter than he intended . . . and I half-cross batted it straight back past him. It was four from the moment I hit it, and I reckon my arms were in the air in triumph before the ball reached the boundary. Then the cameras started flashing, the fans were cheering, my team-mates came out to congratulate me, I had interviews to give, phone calls to answer, no time to ponder . . .

To this point in my life I'd been wary of the 'spotlight'. Now I could no longer avoid it, and for the first time in my life discovered what it was like to be instantaneously recognised by *everybody* wherever you go. It wasn't just the cricket addicts who were saying or pointing or suggesting, 'Isn't that Michael Bevan?' The following day I was the guy on the front page of the morning's paper, the lead on the morning TV and radio news; when I woke up the next morning, I was no longer a name but a celebrity, at least for a little while, and I wasn't sure how to react. I'd never been in that situation before, wasn't naturally comfortable with it, and had no idea how it would pan out. If I came over as embarrassed, that's because that's how I felt.

On the day after I did interviews for 18 radio stations around Australia, plus three TV networks, two current affairs programs and any number of newspapers, here and abroad. Ironically, it seemed the only name I had to compete with for media space was Dean Jones, who'd capped something of a comeback by being selected in the 18-man preliminary Australian squad for the 1996 World Cup, which had been announced during the afternoon of the Windies game. Deano's days in the Test XI were behind him, but he was still considered something of a force in the one-dayers. However, he wasn't selected in the final 14 for the Cup, the selectors preferring to take Test opener Michael Slater. From that day on, it seemed that I took over the role of Australia's No. 1 one-day *specialist* batsman.

It's not my way to chase the limelight. I'm an introvert, I shy away from the cameras, the public appearances. However, as I learnt very quickly after that match-winning boundary against Roger Harper, if you're fair dinkum about playing cricket for Australia—any high-profile sport for Australia—it's something you just have to get used to.

The experience had me admiring my more confident team-mates who usually handle this intense spotlight so well and more often. Though I'd gone on tour with them, and shared experiences, I'd never realised how adept they were at coping with the publicity while still maintaining their excellence on the field. As I have grown older, though, I've probably grown a little more cynical. The fact is that some people do love being in the spotlight, and if you enjoy it, it isn't really too much of a grind, though inevitably there are times when even the biggest media junkie can be overwhelmed by unwanted attention. And, of course, there have been times when sports stars have been carried away by the attention, to the detriment of their performance. One thing I have learnt is that there is no specific right or wrong way to handle the acclaim. It's up to the individual, you've got to work with what you've got. I'm still not 100 per cent comfortable with being a celebrity, but I try to do the best I can.

And I've always got to remember that this weight of celebrity can be misplaced. I had been dropped from the Test team, then scored a hundred for Australia A in a one-dayer against the Poms. Now I'd hit Roger Harper for four. To many observers, I might not have been a Test cricketer, but I was now the master of the late-overs run-chase. I don't think that tag is right, but I can understand how people came to think that way. It's a label that I have never been able to shake, but have learnt to live with.

AUSTRALIA V WEST INDIES, BENSON & HEDGES WORLD SERIES, 1995–96
SYDNEY CRICKET GROUND
1 JANUARY 1996 (50-OVERS MATCH) ▲
TOSS: WEST INDIES

West Indies innings

SC Williams c Healy b Reiffel	5
SL Campbell lbw Warne	15
PV Simmons c Warne b Reiffel	4
S Chanderpaul c Taylor b Reiffel	3
CL Hooper not out	93
JC Adams c Waugh b Warne	0
RA Harper run out	28
OD Gibson b McGrath	4
+CO Browne c Warne b Reiffel	2
CEL Ambrose b Warne	0
*CA Walsh not out	3
Extras (lb 6, w 7, nb 2)	15
Total (9 wickets, 43 overs)	172

Fall: 1-13 (Williams), 2-21 (Simmons), 3-28 (Chanderpaul), 4-54 (Campbell), 5-54 (Adams), 6-135 (Harper), 7-150 (Gibson), 8-164 (Browne), 9-168 (Ambrose)
Bowling: McGrath 9-2-22-1, Reiffel 9-2-29-4, Law 6-0-34-0, Lee 6-0-20-0, Warne 9-2-30-3, Bevan 4-0-31-0

Australia innings

MJ Slater c Simmons b Ambrose	5
*MA Taylor run out	1
ME Waugh c Harper b Gibson	16
RT Ponting b Ambrose	0
SG Law c Browne b Ambrose	10
MG Bevan not out	78
S Lee c Browne b Gibson	0
+IA Healy b Harper	16
PR Reiffel c Hooper b Simmons	34
SK Warne run out	3
GD McGrath not out	1
Extras (lb 2, w 3, nb 4)	9
Total (9 wickets, 43 overs)	173

Fall: 1-4 (Taylor), 2-15 (Slater), 3-15 (Ponting), 4-32 (Law), 5-38 (Waugh), 6-38 (Lee), 7-74 (Healy), 8-157 (Reiffel), 9-167 (Warne)
Bowling: Ambrose 9-3-20-3, Walsh 9-2-22-0, Gibson 9-2-40-2, Harper 8-0-38-1, Simmons 5-0-31-1, Hooper 3-0-20-0

RESULT: AUSTRALIA WON BY ONE WICKET
UMPIRES: PD PARKER AND AJ McQUILLAN
MAN OF THE MATCH: PR REIFFEL

▲ Match reduced to 43 overs per side because of rain

GAME 9

AUSTRALIA V SRI LANKA
BENSON & HEDGES WORLD SERIES
SECOND FINAL
SYDNEY
20 JANUARY 1996

The World Series in 1995–96 continued to be a beauty for me. I actually finished the competition with an average of 194.50, but that was due to the abnormal number of 'not outs' I collected (eight in 10 innings). The finals of that tournament became fairly bitter affairs, as the Sri Lankans—and especially their skipper Arjuna Ranatunga—seemed to decide that they didn't like the way we played our cricket. In Melbourne, Glenn McGrath had a blue with Roshan Mahanama, while in Sydney Ian Healy and Ranatunga became embroiled in a disagreement over whether the Sri Lankan captain was entitled to a runner. Heals' point was that Ranatunga was hardly entitled to a runner just because he was unfit, which seemed to be the Sri Lankan captain's biggest problem. The visitors showed their distaste for us by refusing to shake hands after the match. For me, these disagreements reflected the fact that there are differences in attitude and culture between the various Test-playing nations; inevitably, from time to time, these contrasts are going to lead to conflict.

I have no doubt that many Australians—players, fans and officials—are sometimes guilty of thinking that everyone should play cricket as Australians do. But that's not the way it is. Throughout the world there are different teams that react in different ways to different situations. What is acceptable in Sri Lanka is not necessarily acceptable in Australia. And vice versa. In this case, because the conflict happened on our turf, the mood in our dressing room was that the Sri Lankans should have adapted rather than complained. Perhaps the fact they didn't bend reflected the truth that they were toughening up, becoming more competitive. Also true was the fact that the events were beaten up by the media. It wasn't actually as ugly as it was made out to be.

I've made a habit of not being involved in on-field disagreements. It's not that I have any major philosophical opposition to being aggressive on the field—and I must confess that I'm one of those blokes who thinks that there is a place for sledging in the game, so long as it doesn't degenerate into abuse—but it is not in my nature to get into confrontations, especially not public confrontations.

However, when I was young I did suffer from what my team-mates liked to call 'Bev attacks'. What were they? They were disagreements that concerned only myself, not anyone else. The former NSW selector Neil Marks, in his book *Tales For All Seasons*, sums them up pretty well:

> *Bev attacks were spasmodic and they varied in intensity but none were pleasant to behold. They usually began just after Michael Bevan was dismissed and smouldered away as he walked from the crease and reached the exit, where the lava of recrimination would begin to rush up from the depths of the spleen and hurtle towards the surface. It was then a very tense period for those who knew what was happening. Would the explosion occur before he reached the locker room or after he had slammed the door?*

I can assure Neil that even at my angriest I was able to hold things together reasonably well until I reached the sanctuary of the dressing room. But sometimes, I concede, not much further. Neil continued on to tell the story of one such 'attack':

The Blues were playing Tasmania at Bellerive Oval and the wicket had been playing tricks, causing the Blues upper order to fold quickly, with the exception of Michael Bevan. Bevan played an innings of confidence and maturity and it seemed to those of us watching that he was batting on an entirely different pitch from that of his team-mates. He had almost steered his team to a comfortable position and was heading for a century himself, when he received a rising ball on the leg stump. He intended to pull it to fine leg, but at the last instant he lifted his bat high and let the ball fly past, brushing his shirt as it did. The ball then carried through to the keeper who threw it in the air and screamed an appeal. To everybody's surprise, Bevan was given out caught behind. As he walked from the crease I could see him snorting and I knew it was only a matter of time before smoke began to come out of his ears, for precedent had shown that we were heading for a Bev attack which could probably reach as high as ten on the Richter scale.

I left the viewing room and walked down to the gate, leaned against the fence and gazed serenely into the distance as Bev walked towards the exit. I very much doubt that he knew I was there because his eyes were glazed and the molten aggression suddenly exploded as he reached the gate. At the same time as he slammed the gate, the expletives began, reaching a crescendo when he walked into the Blues' room. I followed him down the ramp into the room which, with the benefit of hindsight, I realise was one of the bravest things I have ever done.

'Expletive, that was the worst expletive decision I've ever had. I went nowhere near the expletive ball. Expletive, expletive, expletive!' yelled Bevan. He then picked up his bat and hurled it across the room.

As well as being a superb batsman Bevan has one of the best arms in the game and the bat whistled across the room and crashed against the manager's old bag which I had left on top of the locker. The bat hit the bag right on its end. The bag seemed to hang in the air for a moment and then spun almost in slow motion to the floor below—like a fat diver doing a one and a half with pike. 'That expletive umpire can go and get expleted,' he shouted, ignoring his brilliant throw, 'and so can that expletive keeper, the expletive little expletive.'

'OK, Bev, that's enough,' I called.

'Expletive, expletive,' he screamed.

'That's enough, Bev,' I yelled.

There was silence for a moment and then trying to sound fatherly, I said, 'Now calm down, go and pick up your bat and stop the language. Bev, you have got to realise that there are spectators just outside the room who can hear every word you're saying.'

He walked over to where his bat was lying near the old bag. He slowly picked up the bat and with a cover-drive action of which Neil Harvey would have been proud, he smashed it against the bag. Then he looked directly at me and I saw the pain in his eyes as he said, 'And they can go and get expleted as well.'

Anyway, enough of that; back to the Sri Lanka matches. They weren't very pleasant, and like all matches in which there are a succession of 'incidents' there was fault on both sides. The Sri Lankans had adopted something of a siege mentality, seeing provocation in everything that happened to them while at the same time seeming happy to provoke trouble whenever they had the chance.

We began the second final with a bang—Mark Taylor and Mark Waugh took 135 runs from the first 25 overs, an effort that came just eight days after the same pair had started a one-day innings in Perth with a partnership of 189. Junior made 130 at the WACA, then 73 in this second final, and stayed at the top of the Australian one-day batting line-up until he was left out of the team for our tour of South Africa in 2002. His move up the order came about mainly to accommodate the return from injury of Steve Waugh to the one-day side. With Stuey Law in brilliant form and people still talking about my innings on New Year's Day, Michael Slater was the unlucky bloke to miss out. Ironically, Tubby was quoted in the press as saying that Slats was a 'more reliable long-term proposition' than a non-regular opener such as Junior. As history shows, the one-day game was actually going in a different direction from how our captain saw it, with many Test batsmen (and bowlers, too) to be asked to play different roles in the one-day game.

For as long as I've known him, Mark Waugh has scored his runs with so little effort. Very graceful, never flustered, he relies on timing and his wonderful balance. Because he's so balanced and flexible, a well-bowled ball to everyone else can be an easy ball to him, without him ever having to do anything outlandish such as charging the bowler or giving himself room by stepping away to the legside. The ability to put a relatively good ball away is a very important and very rare one in the limited-overs game, and it has meant that, as an opener, Mark often doesn't have to bat too differently in one-day cricket from how he bats in a Test match.

Mark is also, of course, a magnificent fieldsman, surely one of the greatest catchers of all time. It's interesting to compare him to other brilliant catchers and fieldsmen, such as Ricky Ponting. 'Punter' works very, very hard on his fielding, sees it as a big part of his game, whereas Mark Waugh does the work, but not any extra work; it's like his batting—he's naturally balanced, sees the ball early and relies on his instincts. Which works for him brilliantly.

After the two Marks' bright opening in this final against Sri Lanka, we lost our way somewhat in the middle order, but accelerated again to reach 5–273. Heals was terrific, hitting 40 from 32 balls at the death, and he and I added 63 from the final 47 balls of the innings.

Then a cyclone blew over during the dinner break, and the Sri Lankans' task was reduced to 168 from 25 overs, which is actually easier than 274 from 50 because, with all 10 wickets still in hand, you can take more risks to keep the run-rate going, while our best bowlers were limited to bowling only five overs each. The wet track made gripping the ball difficult (Warney said later that he only tried to spin two leg-breaks, but still took 3–20 from his five overs), and for much of the night it seemed we might be going to a third final. But when Ranatunga was out in the 21st over, having batted cleverly but sadly having made more of a mark with his gamesmanship, their challenge petered out and we snuck home with eight runs to spare.

The only time I've ever been part of an on-field spat actually involved the great West Indies left-hander Brian Lara, in a one-day international during the 2000–01 Australian season. It was all very innocuous, but still rated a mention in some media reports. All that happened was that Lara, who was fielding while I was batting, walked passed me and said something about me 'getting another not out'. My immediate reaction was to think, 'Oh, OK, he's dirty on the fact that I've been successful in the one-dayers even though I haven't made a lot of runs in Test cricket.' Now I reckon that if everyone was batting at their peak, Brian Lara would probably be the best of them because he can do the most awesome things with the blade, but he can be a prickly fellow, and I couldn't think of any other reason for him to have a go at me. Maybe he was frustrated because he wasn't going as well as he could. We'd played against each other often enough for him not to be suddenly trying to sledge me off my game.

So I just let it go. Then I hit one out to him at cover, and I could have sworn that he threw the ball back at me. That's what his body language suggested. We weren't attempting a run, he wasn't under pressure to do anything with the ball, but he threw it as hard as he could in my direction and I wasn't near the stumps. Maybe my impressions were right, maybe they were wrong. Whatever. Again, I thought, just let it go. Don't let yourself get distracted.

I thought I'd get my chance to reply when he batted. When he was struck on the helmet, I couldn't resist saying something to the effect of, 'That's right, Brian, back and across, back and across', as he practised his technique in an attempt to show that the blow hadn't rattled him. It was a nothing jibe, which reflected the fact that I'm not the king of the one-liners. But he couldn't handle it. He rushed down the wicket to meet me at mid-on and ask where I had been during the Test series. Now, he hadn't had a particularly terrific Test series, so I pointed out that for a lot of the time he'd been in the same place I'd been—off the field not scoring a run. Unfortunately, that fired him up, and he smacked a quickfire 30. For a while it seemed my sledge might turn the game, but after he was dismissed the game settled down and we won fairly comfortably in the end.

Why Lara targeted me that day, I'm still not sure. And I don't really care. It was all harmless. I'm from the school that says leave 99 per cent of what happens on the field out on the field, because they are things that occur in the heat of battle. And I have no doubt that they have been occurring in the heat of battle for a long, long time. There are rare occasions when individuals do go over the top, and when they do they need to be brought into line. But for the rest, let's keep things in perspective.

AUSTRALIA V SRI LANKA, BENSON & HEDGES WORLD SERIES SECOND FINAL, 1995–96
SYDNEY CRICKET GROUND
20 JANUARY 1996 (50-OVERS MATCH) ▲
TOSS: SRI LANKA

Australia innings

ME Waugh c & b Kalpage	73
*MA Taylor c Kaluwitharana b Kalpage	82
RT Ponting c Vaas b Dharmasena	17
SR Waugh c Kalpage b Dharmasena	2
SG Law b Vaas	21
MG Bevan not out	32
+IA Healy not out	40
Extras (lb 5, w 1)	6
Total (5 wickets, 50 overs)	273

DNB: PR Reiffel, SK Warne, CJ McDermott, GD McGrath
Fall: 1-135 (ME Waugh), 2-170 (Ponting), 3-176 (SR Waugh), 4-184 (Taylor), 5-210 (Law)
Bowling: Vaas 10-1-47-1, Pushpakumara 8-1-39-0, Munasinghe 4-0-33-0, Dharmasena 10-0-45-2, Kalpage 10-0-47-2, Jayasuriya 8-0-57-0

Sri Lanka innings

ST Jayasuriya c McGrath b Warne	30
+RS Kaluwitharana lbw McGrath	0
PA de Silva c Reiffel b ME Waugh	6
AP Gurusinha c Warne b Reiffel	24
*A Ranatunga c Law b Warne	41
RS Kalpage c Taylor b McDermott	9
HP Tillakaratne run out	25
HDPK Dharmasena c SR Waugh b Warne	7
AMN Munasinghe not out	3
WPUJC Vaas not out	8
Extras (lb 3, w 3)	6
Total (8 wickets, 25 overs)	159

DNB: KR Pushpakumara
Fall: 1-1 (Kaluwitharana), 2-22 (de Silva), 3-49 (Jayasuriya), 4-66 (Gurusinha), 5-87 (Kalpage), 6-135 (Ranatunga), 7-146 (Dharmasena), 8-146 (Tillakaratne)
Bowling: McGrath 5-0-36-1, ME Waugh 5-0-31-1, Warne 5-0-20-3, SR Waugh 1-0-14-0, Reiffel 4-0-22-1, McDermott 5-0-33-1

RESULT: AUSTRALIA WON BY EIGHT RUNS (REVISED TARGET)
AUSTRALIA WINS THE BEST-OF-THREE FINALS 2–0
UMPIRES: PD PARKER AND SG RANDELL
MEN OF THE FINALS: MA TAYLOR AND SK WARNE

▲ Sri Lanka's target was reduced to 168 from 25 overs

GAME 10

AUSTRALIA V WEST INDIES
WORLD CUP SEMI-FINAL
CHANDIGARH
14 MARCH 1996

After those World Series finals in Australia against Sri Lanka in 1995–96, matters unrelated to cricket took hold, circumstances that threw our preparations for the 1996 World Cup–to be held in India, Pakistan and Sri Lanka–into disarray. Some of the guys in the team received death threats, and an explosion in the centre of Colombo killed a large number of innocent bystanders, after which the Australian Cricket Board (ACB) decided that we wouldn't be going to Sri Lanka for the matches we were scheduled to play there.

The result was that for the first few weeks of our World Cup tour we were basically in limbo. We arrived in Calcutta on 10 February, the opening ceremony was the following day, and then we moved onto Bombay on 14 February. It was only on the previous evening, before we left Calcutta, that we learnt what our schedule for the next week would be–six days in Bombay before we moved on to Visakhapatnam to play Kenya in what would be our first match of the tournament. In the meantime, our opponents would be playing seriously competitive matches while we'd be training and practising among ourselves.

What made a dreadful situation almost tolerable was the ever-present passion of the Indian people for cricket in general and this tournament in particular. While we were sick of the politics and tired of what we thought was an unfair public relations campaign mounted against us by some sections of the Sri Lankan community, we never tired of the way the cricket fan on the street in India welcomed us. Their love for the game is unbelievable; a tad stifling at times, as they can get overexcited at the thought of being close to their heroes, but still always a big positive, especially at times like that when we were a bit dispirited. It's something that hits you, as soon as you arrive in India, just how many people are cricket crazy. The airport in Calcutta is about 25 kilometres from the centre of the city, where our hotel was located, and I reckon we had people lining the streets about 10 deep, all the way from the airport to the foyer. The fervour never let up, not until we left India a few weeks later to go to Lahore for the final.

Whenever you arrive at a new hotel during a tour of India you know that you are going to encounter any number of situations to test your humour. One of the first is being swamped by autograph hunters in the hotel foyer. Indeed, such is the tumult caused by the team's arrival, it gets to the point where it is nearly impossible to sign anything at all. However, signing autographs for fans is part and parcel of the game and most times you try to accommodate the people who want them as best you can.

Sometimes, though, it gets to the stage where things are just about out of control, because of the sheer number of frenzied autograph hunters. You notice that there are more security guards than there are fans and you wonder what they could all possibly be doing. You only find out when you ask them to help you out, and rather than escorting you through the crowd they place another autograph book in front of your face. At times such as this all you can do is run for the safety of your room. But even when you get there the onslaught continues, as you are likely to receive between five and 15 knocks on the door—from people as diverse as room service, housekeeping, maintenance—all enquiring about your needs, but also, coincidentally, all carrying autograph books.

When we did finally get on the field in the 1996 World Cup, we played pretty well, beating Kenya, India and Zimbabwe but losing to the West Indies in Jaipur, after Richie Richardson made 93 not out. My scores for the tournament to this point were: 12, 6 (run out), did not bat and 2 (run out). In the quarter-final against New Zealand, which we won largely because of some superb batting by Mark and Steve Waugh and Stuart Law, I contributed another DNB. At least I'd bowled 25 overs (taking three priceless wickets for 132 runs). In short, I went into the semi-final against the West Indies having hardly had a dig at all. Out in the middle, I'd faced the grand total of 20 balls.

The tournament itself, if you could forget the off-field politics and threats during the preliminaries (which wasn't easy), was fascinating. This was the tournament in which the Sri Lankans introduced us to their cavalier approach to the first 15 overs. Whereas previously, teams had used the opening overs as a means of getting an innings established, the Sri Lankan openers—Sanath Jayasuriya and Romesh Kaluwitharana—attacked from the very first ball, which on the small grounds and slow but true pitches worked a treat. With the ball, they relied to a large degree on their spinners, including part-timers Jayasuriya and Aravinda de Silva (who was also the batsman of the tournament), putting the onus on the opposing batsmen to really hit the ball on the slower pitches. As captain, Ranatunga was as cunning and clever as ever.

It will be noted in years to come that this was a period in cricket's long history when the one-day game advanced, when innovation really came to the fore. I know shrewd thinkers had been devising clever game plans during the previous decade—the work of Allan Border and Bob Simpson at the 1987 World Cup and New Zealand's Martin Crowe in 1992 come to mind—but such was the previously unheralded Sri Lankan success that every team in the world took note that if they were genuinely fresh in their approach to the game then they could match the supposed big guns. Which meant the big guns needed to be resourceful as well if they wanted to stay in front.

Sub-continent teams are very good at playing on their own soil, as good as Australia is these days at playing in Australia. Sri Lanka's victory in the 1996 World Cup was an excellent example of this, so were India's Test defeats of Australia in 1998 and 2001. In the 1996 Cup, India knocked Pakistan out, then Sri Lanka knocked India out; I'm not convinced any team from outside Asia could have beaten those teams in those conditions.

I didn't bat in the quarter-finals even though we finished four wickets down because Tubby Taylor decided to use a 'pinch hitter' in Shane Warne during the middle stages of our run-chase. We needed 287, and Warney went in at the fall of the second wicket, at 2–84, when Steve Waugh would normally have entered. The ploy was extremely successful, because Warney and Mark Waugh added 43 for the third wicket in four-and-a-half overs, which got the required run-rate back to a level from which Mark and brother Steve could control the game.

I don't have a problem with the concept of a pinch hitter in one-day cricket. That said, it generally doesn't work, but you can't knock the theory of having someone whose wicket is not as valuable as a specialist batsman's going out to have a go at quickly boosting the run-rate. So long as everyone involved—the not-out batsman in the middle, the pinch hitter himself and the guys being pushed down the order—is comfortable with the move and the pinch hitter is comfortable in the role, why not try it? However, there are players who—when batting at eight, nine or 10—smash the ball naturally, but when they're thrown in at No. 4 they suddenly play like batsmen, too slowly, and defeat the purpose of why they were sent out there in the first place. Like most unorthodox moves, it's a gamble.

In the semi-final, we were put into bat and crashed to 4–15. Here I was walking out to the middle to play one of the most important matches of my life, having not batted for any worthwhile length of time since we'd left Australia five weeks earlier. Stuey Law, my partner at the other end, was in a similar boat, though at least he'd had a chance in the quarter-final, when he scored a crucial 42 not out. Suddenly, we were both in before the 10th over. But the pitch didn't seem too bad, and we decided to play for a score. What I mean by this is that we didn't really aim at anything specific in terms of a total, just that we needed to set the Windies something that would test them. We ended up posting 8–207; early on I would have been satisfied with around 160–170, but gradually, as our partnership continued, we tilted our sights a little higher.

Even though Chandigarh was slightly bigger than most Indian grounds, on what had evolved into a typically slow but reliable sub-continent track, a target around 200 would not usually have been enough. But sometimes in one-day cricket, a small score can quickly become an imposing one, and with the added pressure that comes with a semi-final of the World Cup, the Windies' innings disintegrated on them. From the moment Steve Waugh bowled Brian Lara, the key batsman, to make it 2–93, we sensed we had a chance, and when Glenn McGrath knocked over Shivnarine Chanderpaul to make it 3–165 in the 42nd over, we moved into overdrive. We became relentless, which I believe caused our opponents to panic; it was as if they expected us to lie down and when we didn't, they didn't know how to win.

Mark Taylor called it 'the greatest escape, by a long way'. Richie Richardson, the West Indies captain, said it was 'awful, really awful'. After Roger Harper was lbw to McGrath, to make it 4–173, Tubby brought back Warney when many captains would have stuck to pace, and the champion spinner took three wickets in three overs. The captain's logic was simple: we needed to bowl them out and Warney was the most likely person to do that. As well, he revealed later, he remembered Otis Gibson, their all-rounder, hitting a 50 against us at the Gabba during the previous World Series competition and thought he was liable to swing indiscriminately against leg-spin. First ball of the new spell, Gibson slashed wildly at a leg-break and was caught behind.

It was a night of many heroes for us, but chief among them was Damien Fleming, who bowled the final over, at the start of which the Windies needed 10 runs and we needed two wickets. Flemo is a terrific one-day bowler because he can change his pace so judiciously—and disguise it so well—he can bowl a quicker one, the yorker, and he can swing the ball, too. And, as he proved here and would do again at the 1999 World Cup, he's the right man for a crisis, very calm and very sensible. Ambrose was run out, Walsh was bowled, and we were through to the final, with three balls and five runs to spare.

My memories of the 1996 Cup final are mostly bad. The Sri Lankans, who had beaten India in the first semi a day before we got through, had an extra day to prepare for the game, which proved significant. We left for Lahore as quickly as we could after the semi-final victory, but still didn't get to train under the lights before the game. If we had, we would have learnt that the dew at night is excessive, leaving the ball soaked to the point of being as slippery as a piece of soap. Bowling first, in the afternoon, would have given us a huge advantage, but we won the toss and batted. We scored 7–241 (Taylor 74, Ponting 45, Bevan 36 not out), good but not brilliant considering we'd been 1–134 after 25 overs. I still thought we were a big chance, considering that Sri Lanka were inexperienced at the highest level, and sometimes any score in a final is good enough. But when we bowled, Warney couldn't grip the ball, while the Sri Lankan batsmen, especially de Silva, were superb. We lost by seven wickets.

Even though we had the worst of the conditions in the final, in the end we were beaten so decisively that we could hardly complain that we were unlucky. The Sri Lankans had a magnificent tournament, and fully deserved their win, for both their skill as cricketers and for the impressive manner in which they carried out their innovative game plans. For me, even though the opportunities to shine were few, I was grateful to have been a part of it all. Today, I have been part of two World Cups and they've both been awesome experiences. The games are 'pressure-cookers', and feature a greater intensity than all other one-day internationals. They mean more to the players and the fans. World Cups seem to accentuate everything that's good about the limited-overs game, and because of that you are guaranteed that the best teams will prevail.

Cut-throat cricket does that.

AUSTRALIA V WEST INDIES, WORLD CUP SEMI-FINAL, 1996
PUNJAB CA STADIUM, CHANDIGARH
14 MARCH 1996 (50-OVERS MATCH)
TOSS: AUSTRALIA

Australia innings

ME Waugh lbw Ambrose	0
*MA Taylor b Bishop	1
RT Ponting lbw Ambrose	0
SR Waugh b Bishop	3
SG Law run out	72
MG Bevan c Richardson b Harper	69
+IA Healy run out	31
PR Reiffel run out	7
SK Warne not out	6
Extras (lb 11, w 5, nb 2)	18
Total (8 wickets, 50 overs)	207

DNB: DW Fleming, GD McGrath
Fall: 1-0 (ME Waugh), 2-7 (Taylor), 3-8 (Ponting), 4-15 (SR Waugh), 5-153 (Law), 6-171 (Bevan), 7-186 (Reiffel), 8-207 (Healy)
Bowling: Ambrose 10-1-26-2, Bishop 10-1-35-2, Walsh 10-1-33-0, Gibson 2-0-13-0, Harper 9-0-47-1, Adams 9-0-42-0

West Indies innings

S Chanderpaul c Fleming b McGrath	80
+CO Browne c & b Warne	10
BC Lara b SR Waugh	45
*RB Richardson not out	49
RA Harper lbw McGrath	2
OD Gibson c Healy b Warne	1
JC Adams lbw Warne	2
KLT Arthurton c Healy b Fleming	0
IR Bishop lbw Warne	3
CEL Ambrose run out	2
CA Walsh b Fleming	0
Extras (lb 4, w 2, nb 2)	8
Total (all out, 49.3 overs)	202

Fall: 1-25 (Browne), 2-93 (Lara), 3-165 (Chanderpaul), 4-173 (Harper), 5-178 (Gibson), 6-183 (Adams), 7-187 (Arthurton), 8-194 (Bishop), 9-202 (Ambrose), 10-202 (Walsh)
Bowling: McGrath 10-2-30-2, Fleming 8.3-0-48-2, Warne 9-0-36-4, ME Waugh 4-0-16-0, SR Waugh 7-0-30-1, Reiffel 5-0-13-0, Bevan 4-1-12-0, Law 2-0-13-0

RESULT: AUSTRALIA WON BY FIVE RUNS
UMPIRES: BC COORAY (SL) AND S VENKATARAGHAVAN
MAN OF THE MATCH: SK WARNE

GAME 11

David Boon had announced his retirement during the 1995–96 season, in part at least because he had been left out of the one-day team from the start of that season and didn't feel comfortable about being in one team but not the other. Which meant, of course, that there was an opening in the Test batting line-up, one that I felt I had a strong chance of filling. That opening appeared to be at No. 6, because Ricky Ponting, who had been batting there with Boonie in the team, was now seen as the man to fill the No. 3 spot. My one-day form at No. 6 gave me an advantage, albeit a small one, over my main rivals, guys such as Stuart Law, Darren Lehmann, Justin Langer and Greg Blewett. Nowhere, as far as I could see, was any consideration given to the fact that I could bowl a bit; in fact, of the five main contenders, only Lang could be rated a non-bowler.

I was duly selected for a short pre-season trip to India that, for the team, turned into a disaster. We didn't win a game on the tour, losing five one-dayers and one Test. Incongruously, given the team's poor form, from a runs-perspective my tour wasn't too bad. In the lead-up match to the Test I scored an unbeaten 100 against an Indian Board President's XI. In the Test, in which we were defeated by seven wickets, I made 26 and 33, sharing a partnership of 67 with Steve Waugh in the second innings that gave me a chance to observe close-up the way Stephen countered the Indian spinners. He finished with 67 not out, in four-and-a-half hours, one of the finest defensive batting efforts I've ever seen. During the Test, 213 overs were bowled by spinners, including 18 from the 'part-time' off-spin of Mark Waugh, but I didn't bowl even one delivery. In the one-dayers, I finished third in the tournament averages (behind Mark Taylor and Michael Slater) and second in the aggregates (behind Tubby), scoring 223 runs in five digs.

We arrived back in Australia less than two weeks before the first Test of our home series with the West Indies, but that still gave me time to score 79 and 150 not out against Victoria in Sydney, which just about locked up my Test place. I then went to Hobart to play for an Australian XI against the West Indians and, after Matthew Hayden and Matthew Elliott began the match with a colossal opening partnership, the Windies quicks bounced me and bounced me some more. I made 29, and the journos had a field day, saying I'd be copping bumpers all summer. Having felt I'd be going to Brisbane with an opportunity to cement my Test place, now all the doubts from two years before re-emerged. It was uncanny; as I sat in my hotel room, anxious for my future, nothing had changed.

In the first innings, I was out first ball and the manner of my dismissal couldn't have been worse. Courtney Walsh fired one in short and it popped off the shoulder of my bat to third slip. In the second innings, I was dropped at slip before I scored, took 25 minutes to break my duck, but was in reasonably good touch once I settled in, pulling Curtly Ambrose for a couple of boundaries, before being dismissed for 20 looking for quick runs before a declaration. In the press afterwards, the general consensus seemed to be that I deserved to be dropped.

At the post-match media conference, Mark Taylor was obliged to speak up for me. 'I wouldn't say he's struggling,' Tubby said, when asked if I'd keep my place in the XI. 'I don't care if they're bowling slow or fast, Michael Bevan is a very good batsman. He's just got to find his niche in the game.'

A positive to come out of the game for me was my bowling. Tubby brought me on in their second innings and I took 3–46 from 14 overs, including the wickets of Sherwin Campbell, who made 113, and Carl Hooper.

'I wasn't too sure how they would come out having not bowled for a number of months, but it was probably the best they've come out in a while. It was just one of those days.'

It turned out that it wasn't just one of those days, because for the rest of the series, and on to South Africa straight afterwards, my bowling became something of a constant in the Australian team. No doubt at all, it kept me in the side, and even provided me with my most productive game in Test cricket.

Of course, when I told the press guys that I hadn't been bowling much, and thus wasn't sure how they'd come out, I was referring to my bowling in a match. One of the questions I'm most often asked is, 'Do you work on your leg-spin?' And the answer is, 'All the time.' Because we practise so much nowadays—we're always at the nets— there's always an opportunity to rehearse aspects of your game that may never see the light of day in a game. The thing is, bowling in the match is very different and no matter how often you practise in the nets, you need match time to keep you sharp and boost your confidence.

In Sydney I scored 16 and 52, and took two more wickets, including Hooper again. But in Melbourne I was left out of the side—Greg Blewett had done well in Sydney as a replacement for Steve Waugh and with the MCG pitch favouring seamers the selectors opted to go with him at 6 instead of me. And Blewey did his part, top scoring with 62 in Australia's first innings. I must admit to still being a little dirty about having been omitted, because two new batsmen, opener Matthew Hayden and No. 3 Justin Langer, had been brought into the starting XI, replacing the injured Matthew Elliott and dropped Ricky Ponting. After Australia lost by six wickets in three days, the two teams then moved on to Adelaide, more of a spinner's deck, and I came back into the side to bat at No. 7 and, as it turned out, bowl first change. Paul Reiffel was named 12th man, with Blewey the closest thing we had to a third seamer.

I can vividly remember a conversation with Steve Waugh I had around this time. I was explaining just how much work I'd done—practising, practising and practising some more against the short stuff in the nets even though I wasn't sure I had a problem in that area—and how I was constantly trying to perfect my technique. I felt I was a bit stiff to be left out in Melbourne, reckoned I'd batted OK in the first two Tests, and that the critics who were bagging me didn't know what they were talking about. And Steve responded by saying that he wasn't sure if that was the right approach. 'I reckon what you need to do,' he said bluntly, 'is be honest with yourself.'

Steve had identified what my problem was, even if I wasn't perceptive enough to recognise it myself. Ridiculously, I didn't listen to him. Nothing in my mental make-up had really changed from the previous time I'd played Test cricket. I'd scored a couple of 20s, a 50 and a duck, and never looked like going on to get a big score. Maybe I was *too* motivated, *too* keen to succeed?

It is an undeniable fact—something I have learnt now, the hard way—that one of the most vital aspects of being a top-class athlete is to relax and just play. At Test level, especially at home when you're not sure of yourself and your place in the side, any little doubts get exposed. It can be bloody hard to stay loose, to just be yourself. Instead, there is a real temptation to be distracted by your own and others' expectations. To say people aren't mentally strong enough to succeed in Test cricket implies that they are weak, but I don't think they are weak so much as lacking focus and not knowing what works for them. In my case, I didn't understand what was needed mentally to perform at my best. Test cricket tested me out and I failed. I don't think I'd fail if I sat that test again.

I went into that fourth Test extremely nervous about being a frontline bowler. 'He's our second-best spinner at the moment,' said Mark Taylor in the pre-match media conference. 'If it's a dry-looking wicket, where I don't think three quicks are going to be necessary, with the likes of Stephen Waugh and Greg Blewett in the side, we may well go with a quick missing out. In 1993 [when Australia won an Ashes series in England 4–1], our two spinners were Shane Warne and Tim May. This time they would be Shane Warne and Michael Bevan. The added bonus would be that Michael Bevan's a good batsman as well.'

While my captain might have been optimistic, my expectations were low. Frankly, I just wanted to get out of the game without embarrassing myself. Instead, I went out and took 10 wickets. It was surreal. 'Not since his ankle-biter days had Bevan been chosen primarily as a bowler,' wrote Peter Roebuck in the *Sydney Morning Herald*, 'but he did not freeze, and his googlies were too much for a swinging tail.' In fact, my victims did not only include tail enders, but also Campbell, Shivnarine Chanderpaul and Jimmy Adams.

'I'm not Shane Warne, I'm not a full-time spinner,' I told the media at a press conference at the end of one of the day's play. 'I'm someone who is a wicket taker; I'll bowl 10 or 15 overs in a day and if I pick up a couple of wickets then great . . .'

And it was great, though getting 10 wickets in a Test before I scored a Test hundred was actually something of a sore point for me. So I made it known in all the interviews I did that I wasn't bowling too well, which wasn't true—they were fizzing out all right and the Windies batsmen couldn't pick my wrong 'un—but I wanted to be known as a batsman. Consequently I didn't enjoy my bowling success, or the fact that I was fooling Test-class batsmen, as much as I should have. Still, the wickets meant I was going to keep my place in the side, and I actually scored 85 not out in the fourth Test and 87 not out and 15 in the fifth. In the first match, I batted slowly, but I thought I went OK. There was some criticism of how long it took for my runs to accumulate, but I dismissed that as coming from people who wanted me to bat as they wanted to, how they'd seen me bat in the one-dayers.

My bowling was always more effective against blokes who couldn't pick the googly. And the Windies didn't have a clue, which meant I could land it just about anywhere without the batsmen being able to score. I was lucky in that Warney looked after Brian Lara in both innings, and the rest of them were too indecisive.

My favourite delivery from this Test was the one that got Chanderpaul in the second innings. I rely on the wrong 'un to get most of my wickets, because most guys can't pick it. I don't get a heap of wickets with what I call my 'normal leg-spinner' (which is actually an off-spinner to right-handers, but it's bowled the same way as leg-spinners are explained in the coaching books, which are always written by right–handers). I was on as early as the 12th over, and early in my third over I got a leg-break exactly right and pushed a surprised Chanderpaul right back onto his stumps. Next ball was pitched up to the left-hander, in the perfect spot where he had to reach forward tentatively for it on an off-stump line, and he sliced it to Mark Taylor at first slip. I didn't beat him with subterfuge; rather, it was the fact that the ball was perfectly pitched and turned enough to nick the outside edge of his bat.

Twenty runs later, I had Campbell caught at slip as well, this time the ball buzzing and bouncing the other way. The West Indies were 3–42, still 345 runs from making us bat again. They wouldn't recover, and the following day the match was over, one of Australia's biggest ever wins against the West Indies. And I was ushered to the presentation area to receive the man-of-the-match award. I just wished that when I was asked about my efforts during the game, the questions might have focused a little bit more on my batting.

AUSTRALIA V WEST INDIES, FOURTH TEST, 1996–97
ADELAIDE OVAL
25–28 JANUARY 1997
TOSS: WEST INDIES

West Indies first innings

SL Campbell c Healy b McGrath	0
AFG Griffith lbw Bichel	13
S Chanderpaul c Taylor b Warne	20
BC Lara c Blewett b Warne	9
CL Hooper c ME Waugh b McGrath	17
JC Adams c & b Warne	10
+JR Murray c Blewett b Bevan	34
IR Bishop c Healy b Bevan	1
*CA Walsh c Healy b Bevan	0
CE Cuffy c Healy b Bevan	2
PIC Thompson not out	10
Extras (b 4, lb 1, nb 9)	14
Total (all out, 47.5 overs)	130

Fall: 1-11 (Campbell), 2-22 (Griffith), 3-45 (Lara), 4-58 (Chanderpaul), 5-72 (Hooper), 6-113 (Adams), 7-117 (Murray), 8-117 (Walsh), 9-119 (Cuffy), 10-130 (Bishop)
Bowling: McGrath 12-4-21-2, Bichel 10-1-31-1, Bevan 9.5-2-31-4, Warne 16-4-42-3

Australia first innings

*MA Taylor lbw Bishop	11
ML Hayden st Murray b Hooper	125
JL Langer c Murray b Cuffy	19
ME Waugh c Murray b Hooper	82
SR Waugh c Hooper b Chanderpaul	26
GS Blewett b Cuffy	99
MG Bevan not out	85
+IA Healy c Lara b Thompson	12
SK Warne c Hooper b Bishop	9
AJ Bichel c Lara b Walsh	7
GD McGrath b Walsh	1
Extras (b 2, lb 15, w 4, nb 20)	41
Total (all out, 162.3 overs)	517

Fall: 1-35 (Taylor), 2-78 (Langer), 3-242 (ME Waugh), 4-288 (Hayden), 5-288 (SR Waugh), 6-453 (Blewett), 7-475 (Healy), 8-494 (Warne), 9-507 (Bichel), 10-517 (McGrath)
Bowling: Walsh 37.3-6-101-2, Bishop 34-6-92-2, Cuffy 33-4-116-2, Thompson 16-0-80-1, Hooper 31-7-86-2, Adams 8-0-23-0, Chanderpaul 3-1-2-1

West Indies second innings

SL Campbell	c Taylor b Bevan	24
AFG Griffith	c SR Waugh b McGrath	1
S Chanderpaul	c Taylor b Bevan	8
BC Lara	c Healy b Warne	78
CL Hooper	lbw Warne	45
JC Adams	c ME Waugh b Bevan	0
IR Bishop	c Bevan b Warne	0
+JR Murray	c Taylor b Bevan	25
*CA Walsh	c SR Waugh b Bevan	1
CE Cuffy	not out	3
PIC Thompson	c Hayden b Bevan	6
Extras	(b 2, lb 5, nb 6)	13
Total	(all out, 69.4 overs)	204

Fall: 1-6 (Griffith), 2-22 (Chanderpaul), 3-42 (Campbell), 4-138 (Hooper), 5-145 (Adams), 6-154 (Bishop), 7-181 (Lara), 8-192 (Walsh), 9-196 (Murray), 10-204 (Thompson)
Bowling: McGrath 17-4-31-1, Bichel 8-4-16-0, Bevan 22.4-3-82-6, Warne 20-4-68-3, Blewett 2-2-0-0

Close of play

Day 1: Australia 2-139 (Hayden 66*, ME Waugh 31*)
Day 2: Australia 5-434 (Blewett 91*, Bevan 47*)
Day 3: West Indies 6-154 (Lara 65*)

RESULT: AUSTRALIA WON BY AN INNINGS AND 183 RUNS
UMPIRES: SG RANDELL AND DR SHEPHERD (ENG)
MAN OF THE MATCH: MG BEVAN

GAME 12

AUSTRALIA V SOUTH AFRICA
SECOND TEST
PORT ELIZABETH
14–17 MARCH 1997

For the fifth Test of the Windies series, at the traditionally pace-bowling-friendly WACA Ground in Perth, the selectors left Justin Langer out and promoted Greg Blewett up the order, so an extra fast bowler could be included and the man of the match from Adelaide could bat at No. 6. We lost the game by 10 wickets in three days, but retained the satisfaction of being the first Australian side to win a series against the men from the Caribbean in Australia for 21 years.

Curtly Ambrose set up that fifth Test victory by taking five wickets in the first innings, and Courtney Walsh took five in the second innings. They were both superb practitioners, but if I had to pick one I'd go for Walsh. I'm basing that choice purely on how I found them, and I should stress that I don't think I ever faced Ambrose at his absolute peak. Everyone who did have the misfortune to do that insists that he was the best, but I found Walsh harder to play because of his angle of delivery. With Ambrose, I felt as if I knew where every delivery was going to be: just short of a length, in at the hip area, don't expect to score much, with the odd bouncer thrown in. Walsh was also hard to score off, but he varied his line and length more, and coming from that wide angle, for a leftie like me he was always testing you. When you add the fact that Walsh was so good for so long, to the point that when he retired he'd taken 85 more wickets than anyone else in the game's history, in my eyes he was just about unbelievable.

Mark Taylor scored 2 and 1 in that Perth Test, completing an average series for him in which he had managed to make just 153 runs in the five Tests, including 47 runs in his most recent six innings. As his bad run continued, speculation mounted as to whether Tubby would retain his place in the side. And as this conjecture simmered, and threatened to boil over, I gradually became embroiled in the debate. Throughout the Test series that followed in South Africa, whether the wicket was turning or seaming, I batted at No. 7 and was the fourth bowler, which led to strong suggestions from a number of observers that I was there as an extra batsman, to protect Mark Taylor, as much as I was in as a bowler.

Tubby hadn't scored many runs, but he was captain and a great captain at that, so he stayed in the team, which I'm sure was fair enough. But keeping Tubby in the team and me as a frontline bowler— both selections that could be questioned, and were quite stridently in the media—did allow the perception to grow that not everyone in the squad was being treated equally. There is no doubt that I was getting chosen as a spinner on tracks that were more suited to seamers, but the team had been winning consistently, and it wasn't for me to judge whether my continued selection was the right or wrong decision; my job was to try to play as well as I could. But the continuing conjecture did create a bit of unrest in the team, not so much by impacting on players' performances—I think, once the teams were chosen, the guys still put in 100 per cent and in most cases played well—but by creating an unsettled environment that damaged the team chemistry.

As a general rule—and I don't think it matters what the situation is or who is involved—I believe players perform at their best when there is a high degree of consistency when it comes to the way players are treated and the manner in which teams are selected. You can never

Left: My first experience of the 'big time'—with Australian Prime Minister Bob Hawke after the PM's XI defeated the Pakistanis in Canberra in January 1990. (Courtesy of the Bevan Family)

Below: I would never have believed I could get this far down the track. Award-winning photographer Tim Clayton took this shot during my hundred for New South Wales against Queensland at the SCG in March 1991. The keeper is Peter Anderson. (Tim Clayton/Sydney Morning Herald)

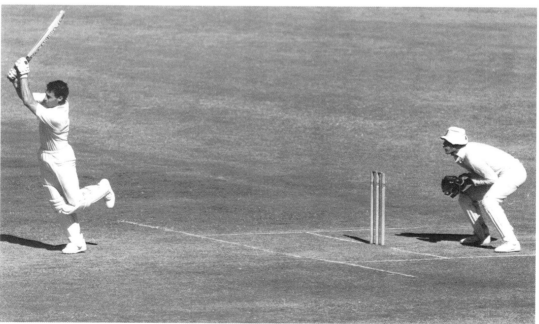

Top: Two images from my first Test innings, against Pakistan in Karachi in 1994. Left: A pull shot against the Pakistani pace attack. Right: Reaching 50 on my way to 82. (Getty Images)

Bottom: Within three months of my debut, Test cricket suddenly seemed so much harder. Here, the English celebrate my downfall—caught Atherton bowled Gough 3—in Melbourne during the second Test of the 1994–95 Ashes series. (Getty Images)

Above: A famous night. I've just hit the West Indies' Roger Harper for four—off the last possible ball of the match—to win a one-day international at the SCG on New Year's Day 1996. No. 11 Glenn McGrath moves in to share the moment. (Steve Christo/ Sydney Morning Herald)

Left: Facing Damien Fleming in the nets at Lahore before the 1996 World Cup final. (Getty Images)

Above: I've just dismissed Jimmy Adams, caught by Mark Waugh for a duck, in the West Indies' second innings of the fourth Test of 1996–97, in Adelaide. This was one of 10 wickets I took during the match. (Getty Images)

Right: Bowling for Australia at Old Trafford during the third Test of the 1997 Ashes series. (Getty Images)

The 1999 World Cup was one of the most exciting times of my career.

Left: A drive through mid-on during my innings of 65 in the semi-final against South Africa at Edgbaston. (Getty Images)

Below: A mad dash off the field after our great escape—a tie after South African No. 11 Allan Donald was sensationally run out—won us a place in the Cup final. (Getty Images)

Right: With Adam Gilchrist (centre), captain Steve Waugh and the World Cup trophy on the balcony at Lord's after our big win over Pakistan. (Getty Images)

On a surf ski at Coogee Beach as the Australian one-day squad enjoys a change from net practice in January 2000. At the time, the team was in the early stages of a world record sequence of 13 straight one-day international victories. (Getty Images)

Acknowledging the crowd in Melbourne after becoming the first batsman to hit 100 'indoors' during a one-day international. (Getty Images)

A pull shot from Margao during the crucial fifth and final one-dayer against India in April 2001. We won the match by four wickets and the series 3-2. (Getty Images)

Left: Celebrations at the WACA in Perth after the Blues beat Western Australia to win the 2000-01 Mercantile Mutual Cup. (Getty Images)

Below: The scene on the Lord's balcony immediately after I was struck by a can hurled from the crowd during the presentations that followed the 2001 NatWest Series final. While I hold my jaw and try to work out what happened, Mark Waugh points to where he thinks the missile was thrown. (Getty Images)

The comeback victory we stole from New Zealand in a do-or-die one-dayer in January 2002 was one of the most thrilling I've been involved in. **Above:** A drive to long-on during the vital partnership with Brett Lee. **Below left:** Andy Bichel has just hit the winning four, and I can hardly contain my excitement. **Below right:** With Bic as we begin our triumphant walk off the MCG, needing a moment to take in what we've just achieved. (Getty Images)

please everyone all the time, but if you can create an environment in which everyone knows where they stand, and everyone believes they are getting a fair go, then more often than not you'll get the performances you're after.

The case with our captain and his lack of runs was a very rare situation that would have created problems whatever solution was put in place. It wasn't going to be fixed until Tubby started scoring runs again, which didn't happen until later in 1997, in England. Here in South Africa, I was concentrating on trying to take advantage of my opportunity. By this stage, I was bowling really well—I can remember a tour match in Western Province where I bowled 46.4 overs in the game, 29.4 in the second innings, which for me was unheard of—and maybe, just maybe, I was beginning to get used to this all-rounder role. It wasn't a bad batting side I was up against either, in that Western Province match, as it included, among others, Test stars such as Jacques Kallis, Gary Kirsten, Brian McMillan and Herschelle Gibbs. The first Test worked out OK, as it was played on a turner, so we didn't miss the third quick, but the second and third Tests were played on seaming tracks and the strategy of going in with just two fast men was obviously questionable.

As it turned out, we won the series, but maybe we made it a little harder for ourselves than we needed by having me batting at seven and bowling. But I did take six wickets in the first Test (including the last four of the match) and scored 37 not out, as we won by an innings and plenty, and then took another three wickets in the second (all in the second innings, 3–18 from 13 overs) and scored 24 at the death as Mark Waugh played perhaps his finest hand to win us a famous victory.

It's funny how Junior's match-winning innings has been almost forgotten, but it really was outstanding, one of the great ones. After we'd won so decisively on a low, slow wicket in the first Test, the South Africans obviously decided that their best chance of beating us was on a seamer, so despite the fact that our intelligence was that the wicket in Port Elizabeth had been a turner all season, we found ourselves playing the Test on a wicket with a heap of grass on it. Batting was really tough, and after we bowled South Africa out for 209 they came back and knocked us over for just 108. When Kirsten and Adam Bacher reached stumps on the second day at 0–83 in their second innings, effectively 0–184, our chances looked remote at best.

If Tubby had been struggling with the bat, he made up for it now with some inspired leadership. That night he called us all together, to engineer a fightback. In our captain's view, we could still win; what was needed was a refocus—our game plan was still right, we needed to stick to it. We needed to be aggressive, back ourselves, never give up. When Jason Gillespie stepped up the next morning to bowl Kirsten immediately, we were inspired. Three more wickets fell before they passed 100, and our eventual victory target of 270 was around 100 to 150 less than we could have reasonably expected when play had ended the night before. By stumps we'd reached 3–145, and we all walked back from the ground to our hotel, so pumped were we after what Ian Healy later called the 'best day of our careers'.

Scoring anything over 250 in the last innings of a Test match is always very hard to do. You only have to look at the record books to see that it is not done very often. On that type of wicket it is just about impossible, against what was a pretty fair bowling attack led by Allan Donald.

At lunch we still needed 66, with five wickets in hand. I had arrived in the middle just before the break, after Blewey played over one from the spinner, Paul Adams. Back out in the middle, I might have been run out when I dashed through for a 'one-day' single, then Donald struck me on the glove with one that flew off just short of a length, then pitched slightly shorter and wider and I crunched him through extra cover for four. Next over, Mark Waugh went to his hundred—which he later called the best knock of his life—and then was dropped by Cullinan off Donald. The score reached 5–244, still 26 to win.

When that catch went down, it seemed as if South Africa's last chance was gone. We inched to 258—Waugh 116, Bevan 24—and then three wickets fell for seven in 11 balls and the game was alive once more. Junior was the first to fall, bowled by Kallis, and then, next over without another run being scored, I was caught at first slip off Hansie Cronje. I had the pads off and was back in the viewing area in time to see Warney trapped lbw by Kallis. Five to win, two wickets in hand, Gillespie went out to play the biggest short innings of his career.

It's an ugly feeling, sitting in the dressing room or on the balcony watching the action, and there's nothing you can do about it, when just a couple of minutes earlier there *was* something you could do about it. For the guys who had been sitting watching all day, they were caught up in the drama, while I was reflecting on a missed opportunity. In the middle, 'Dizzy' Gillespie played out the rest of Kallis' over, leaving Heals to face Cronje.

Heals defended the first two deliveries; the third was aimed at his pads and he simply swung through the line, connected perfectly and hit it for six. It was a gutsy shot, typical of the bloke's approach to the game. The pandemonium in the room reflected the enormity of the team's achievement; the celebrations would go long into the night. Indeed, two things stick in my mind about this game—one is that mighty post-match party; the other is the crowd that helped make the game so special.

When you have played international cricket for long enough, you know that as an opposition player fielding anywhere near the boundary you're going to cop a fair bit of stick from the crowd. However, I found running the boundary at Port Elizabeth to be an absolute joy. One of the main reasons for this was that one of the sections in the main grandstand was filled by a brass band belting out some terrific tunes. The band started at 11am and didn't finish until we walked off the field at the end of the day. When you field for an entire day, the important thing is to keep yourself keen, fresh and focused. Playing in this kind of environment certainly helps.

The celebrations! One of the great feelings in cricket is winning a tough series or competition. There are inevitably some bad times in a career so it is important to really enjoy the good ones. The fantastic thing about playing a team game is being able to share the experience with the other guys. On this occasion it was Matthew Hayden and Jason

Gillespie who put on a show for the boys. 'Haydos' was the instigator and I think 'Dizzy' got dragged along for the ride. Haydos made up a skit involving the 'hunter' and the 'prey'—the passion and the intensity shown by both players had everyone in stitches and it was the start of one of the best of the many great nights I've been fortunate to share with a winning Australian team.

AUSTRALIA V SOUTH AFRICA, SECOND TEST, 1996–97
ST GEORGE'S PARK, PORT ELIZABETH
14–17 MARCH 1997
TOSS: AUSTRALIA

South Africa first innings

G Kirsten	c Hayden b Gillespie	0
AM Bacher	c Elliott b McGrath	11
JH Kallis	c Blewett b Gillespie	0
DJ Cullinan	c Warne b Gillespie	34
*WJ Cronje	b McGrath	0
HH Gibbs	b Gillespie	31
BM McMillan	c SR Waugh b Warne	55
SM Pollock	lbw Gillespie	0
+DJ Richardson	c McGrath b Warne	47
AA Donald	c & b Warne	9
PR Adams	not out	5
Extras	(b 8, lb 8, w 1)	17
Total	(all out, 74.4 overs)	209

Fall: 1-13 (Kirsten), 2-17 (Kallis), 3-21 (Bacher), 4-22 (Cronje), 5-70 (Cullinan), 6-95 (Gibbs), 7-95 (Pollock), 8-180 (Richardson), 9-204 (McMillan), 10-209 (Donald)
Bowling: McGrath 22-7-66-2, Gillespie 23-10-54-5, Warne 23.4-5-62-3, Blewett 4-2-3-0, Bevan 2-0-8-0

Australia first innings

ML Hayden	c Cullinan b Pollock	0
*MA Taylor	c Richardson b Pollock	8
MTG Elliott	run out	23
ME Waugh	lbw Cronje	20
SR Waugh	c Richardson b McMillan	8
GS Blewett	b Donald	13
MG Bevan	c Richardson b McMillan	0
+IA Healy	c Bacher b Cronje	5
SK Warne	lbw Adams	18
JN Gillespie	not out	1
GD McGrath	c Richardson b Kallis	0
Extras	(b 1, lb 7, w 2, nb 2)	12
Total	(all out, 70.4 overs)	108

Fall: 1-1 (Hayden), 2-13 (Taylor), 3-48 (ME Waugh), 4-64 (Elliott), 5-66 (SR Waugh), 6-70 (Bevan), 7-85 (Healy), 8-86 (Blewett), 9-106 (Warne), 10-108 (McGrath)
Bowling: Donald 23-13-18-1, Pollock 6-3-6-2, Adams 4-0-5-1, McMillan 14-2-32-2, Cronje 14-7-21-2, Kallis 9.4-2-18-1

South Africa second innings

G Kirsten b Gillespie	43
AM Bacher c McGrath b Gillespie	49
JH Kallis run out	2
DJ Cullinan lbw Gillespie	2
*WJ Cronje c Healy b Bevan	27
HH Gibbs c ME Waugh b McGrath	7
BM McMillan lbw Bevan	2
SM Pollock lbw Warne	17
+DJ Richardson not out	3
AA Donald c Warne b Bevan	7
PR Adams c Taylor b Warne	1
Extras (b 1, lb 5, nb 2)	8
Total (all out, 73.4 overs)	168

Fall: 1-87 (Kirsten), 2-98 (Kallis), 3-99 (Bacher), 4-100 (Cullinan), 5-122 (Gibbs), 6-137 (McMillan), 7-152 (Cronje), 8-156 (Pollock), 9-167 (Donald), 10-168 (Adams)
Bowling: McGrath 13-3-43-1, Gillespie 18-4-49-3, SR Waugh 4.3-0-16-0, Blewett 7.3-3-16-0, Warne 17.4-7-20-2, Bevan 13-3-18-3

Australia second innings

*MA Taylor lbw McMillan	13
ML Hayden run out	14
MTG Elliott c & b Adams	44
ME Waugh b Kallis	116
SR Waugh c Cronje b Kallis	18
GS Blewett b Adams	7
MG Bevan c Cullinan b Cronje	24
+IA Healy not out	10
SK Warne lbw Kallis	3
JN Gillespie not out	0
Extras (b 11, lb 8, w 3)	22
Total (8 wickets, 93.3 overs)	271

Fall: 1-23 (Taylor), 2-30 (Hayden), 3-113 (Elliott), 4-167 (SR Waugh), 5-192 (Blewett), 6-258 (ME Waugh), 7-258 (Bevan), 8-265 (Warne)
Bowling: Donald 26-6-75-0, McMillan 21-5-46-1, Cronje 9.3-1-36-1, Kallis 16-7-29-3, Adams 21-4-66-2

Close of play
Day 1: Australia 1-10 (Taylor 7*, Elliott 1*)
Day 2: South Africa 0-83 (Kirsten 41*, Bacher 38*)
Day 3: Australia 3-145 (ME Waugh 54*, SR Waugh 11*)

RESULT: AUSTRALIA WON BY TWO WICKETS
UMPIRES: RE KOERTZEN AND S VENKATARAGHAVAN (IND)
MAN OF THE MATCH: ME WAUGH

GAME 13

AUSTRALIA V SOUTH AFRICA
SIXTH ONE-DAY INTERNATIONAL
CENTURION PARK
10 APRIL 1997

The one-day series that followed the Test matches on our 1997 tour of South Africa was filled with drama and controversy. During the third Test, it was announced that three players—Matthew Elliott, Justin Langer and Matthew Hayden—would not be staying for the one-day series. Stuart Law, Adam Gilchrist, Michael di Venuto, Brendon Julian and Adam Dale were all called into the squad, accelerating the move towards separate Test and one-day squads. Stuey had by now been tagged a one-day cricketer, and sadly I was soon to join him. Then Ian Healy, our vice-captain, was suspended for two one-dayers after he was caught throwing his bat after he was wrongfully given out on the final day of the Test. This threw into chaos a plan for Tubby to skip the one-dayers, and he played the first couple before his deputy returned to take over the captaincy. Glenn McGrath would miss the entire series and Mark Waugh missed a couple of games as well. Yet we won the series, and with some style too.

I remember the South African captain Hansie Cronje, before the one-dayers started, dismissing our side to some degree, saying words to the effect that we had only one top-class one-day batsman (he didn't say which one). It was nice to prove him wrong. At that time, South Africa was generally regarded as the best one-day team in the world—they'd won two of the three tournaments they played in 1996–97, and unluckily lost the final of the other after going through six qualifying matches undefeated—but we still beat them most times we played them. I think that was simply because we had such a high regard for them, which really brought out the best in us.

I had an excellent series, with the highlight being my first one-day century, which came in game six. This was my first hundred in one-day internationals, in my 55th appearance. We were chasing a big total, and fell to 3–58 before Steve Waugh and I became involved in the crucial partnership. At this point we needed 227 from 211 deliveries. And we got them, with five wickets in hand and six balls to spare.

Whenever I am asked about my favourite one-day game or my best innings, I guess most people expect me to bring up the New Year's Day 1996 game against the Windies, or, lately, the game at the MCG against New Zealand in January 2002. But this game is right up there. This was probably the best I've batted over a long period against decent opposition in a crunch one-day match. It was a very important game for us, a chance to claim a seven-game series that we had been outsiders to win when it began. And because I was down to bat at No. 5 and we lost three wickets early in our innings, I had a rare chance to play a long innings.

Because of the quality of the South African attack, I knew we weren't going to get many easy overs. And the required run-rate from the word go was pretty imposing, so I went out there determined to score quickly from the jump. That meant that, instead of going in and ticking the scoreboard over mainly by finding singles, I went out there and played some big shots.

When Tugga first came in, they attacked him with quite a deal of short stuff, and it took him quite a while to get going, not the sort of start you want when you're chasing a big score. Eventually, however, he seemed to decide enough is enough, and he went after them. Donald dropped three short in one over and they all went for four. Then Rudi Bryson was square cut for six. That took the pressure off; it always does when a batsman gets the better of the opposition's premier bowler. The chase was on.

The next defining moment of our innings came at around the 30-over mark, when the required run-rate had climbed up again to around seven an over, and we decided we needed to make a bit of a charge. Derek Crookes was bowling, and we took to him, reviving the run-rate, which meant that we could go through the final 10 overs without having to resort to low-percentage shots to get us home. For the last 15 overs we needed no more than a run a ball, and considering the form we were in, and the mood of the game, we were travelling nicely.

The partnership between Steve and me was worth 189 runs, at the time the biggest fourth-wicket partnership for Australia in one-day international cricket and the equal fourth highest by an Australian pair for any wicket. Our stand was only broken when Tugga was given out lbw to Shaun Pollock, and just before the end, after I'd reached 103 from 93 balls (the first 50 in 54 balls, the next 53 in 39), I copped a shocker to be given out leg-before to Bryson. The ball pitched at least a bat-handle's length outside leg stump, but by then we were nearly home and Heals and Gilly saw us through to a sweet victory.

At the media conference afterwards, Heals stated that he'd never played in a better one-day victory. Then he continued:

'They [Tugga and me] played particularly well. The wicket was great, the outfield was fast, (but) seeing was tough tonight and the ball was getting wet. So it was a fantastic chase under tough conditions.

'I hope I'm not carried away, I don't think I am, but I think that's the best one-day partnership I've witnessed. Bevan's hundred was up there with the best hundreds I've ever seen in one-day cricket.

'He knows his game. He knows when he can score his runs, he's a fantastic runner so he knows he's got the fielders and opposing captain on edge because their field placings have to be spot on. And he's got the ability to hit fours, the flair that we probably haven't seen yet at this level.'

Hansie Cronje also called our stand the best he'd seen. I know it appears arrogant to put these comments down on paper in this book, but as I said, I regard this innings as one of my very best and the stand as a beauty, so I think I'm entitled to play it up. Cronje also stated that I was 'tailor-made' for one-day cricket, because, as he put it, 'Bevan creates angles that are very awkward for the bowlers'.

He continued: 'When he flicks it off his hip there's normally two rather than one. It's very annoying for a captain when you're cutting off boundaries but they're still scoring more than six an over. It's really annoying.'

I took the description 'annoying' as a real compliment. In its own way, that one word captures the way I usually try to bat in one-day games. Once I'd hit those big shots at the start of my innings, to get our run-chase on track, I was able to play the way I like to. You don't necessarily have to keep hitting four after four after four to sustain the run-rate, to keep the winning target in sight.

AUSTRALIA V SOUTH AFRICA, SIXTH ONE-DAY INTERNATIONAL, 1996–97
CENTURION PARK, VERWOERDBURG
10 APRIL 1997 (50-OVERS MATCH)
TOSS: SOUTH AFRICA

South Africa innings

AM Bacher b Dale	15
HH Gibbs c Healy b Gillespie	33
*WJ Cronje run out	80
DJ Cullinan c ME Waugh b Warne	89
JH Kallis st Healy b Warne	3
JN Rhodes run out	10
SM Pollock c Dale b Bichel	33
DN Crookes not out	4
+DJ Richardson not out	0
Extras (lb 12, w 4, nb 1)	17
Total (7 wickets, 50 overs)	284

DNB: RE Bryson, AA Donald
Fall: 1-52 (Bacher), 2-77 (Gibbs), 3-226 (Cronje), 4-232 (Cullinan), 5-232 (Kallis), 6-261 (Rhodes), 7-283 (Pollock)
Bowling: Dale 10-0-44-1, Bichel 9-0-50-1, Warne 10-1-52-2, Gillespie 9-0-45-1, Blewett 5-0-41-0, Bevan 7-0-40-0

Australia innings

ME Waugh c Rhodes b Pollock	0
GS Blewett c Crookes b Pollock	21
SG Law b Cronje	31
SR Waugh lbw Pollock	89
MG Bevan lbw Bryson	103
AC Gilchrist not out	20
*+IA Healy not out	9
Extras (lb 5, w 7, nb 2)	14
Total (5 wickets, 49 overs)	287

DNB: SK Warne, AJ Bichel, AC Dale, JN Gillespie
Fall: 1-0 (ME Waugh), 2-36 (Blewett), 3-58 (Law), 4-247 (Bevan), 5-262 (SR Waugh)
Bowling: Pollock 10-0-40-3, Bryson 10-0-63-1, Donald 10-1-59-0, Cronje 7-0-46-1, Crookes 6-0-37-0, Kallis 6-0-37-0

RESULT: AUSTRALIA WON BY FIVE WICKETS
UMPIRES: DF BECKER AND SB LAMBSON
MAN OF THE MATCH: MG BEVAN

GAME 14

A good test for fans of cricket trivia is to ask who won the limited-overs tournaments that preceded the Test series on the Ashes tours of 1981, 1985, 1989, 1993 and 1997. Only in 1993 did the same team prevail in both the Tests and one-dayers. In 1997, England actually won all three of the one-day internationals, and won them pretty decisively, by six wickets each time. At least the ease of their victory dropped a little with each game—the first match was lost with 9.5 overs to spare, the second with 10 balls still available, the third with the last ball of the 49th over. The English media's response was quite extraordinary; one paper, after the first game, announced proudly in a back-page headline: 'They're Coming Home, They're Coming Home! The Ashes Are Coming Home!'

They weren't. During those very early days of our tour, it was not so much a case of England playing really well as that we played some poor one-day cricket. We went into those three games seriously under-prepared. Taking advantage of any spare time available, we'd all taken it slightly easy after the South African tour, and then seen a succession of rainy days after we arrived in the UK. The opening one-dayer came just a week after our first game of the tour, and I'd managed to score just eight runs in the one innings I'd had. In the first one-day international, I managed to top-score with 30 before being run out, but even after that, when asked if I was in good form, I couldn't give an honest answer. I just hadn't been out in the middle long enough to really know. When we bowled, defending 170, we did manage to reduce England to 4–40, but Graham Thorpe and Adam Hollioake batted superbly and we didn't take another wicket.

At this point, I was looking forward to a big tour. I felt my two seasons in England with Yorkshire could only help me. My batting in my most recent Test matches—late in the West Indies series in Australia (I finished that series, against the best fast bowlers on the planet, with an average of 55) and then the Tests in South Africa—had been reasonable, maybe even better than reasonable. I was thrilled with the way I had batted in the one-dayers in South Africa.

And I was excited to be a part of an Ashes adventure. Being part of an Ashes series—as I had been, albeit unsuccessfully, in 1994–95— had been special. Being on this tour was doubly so. Next to wearing the baggy green for the first time, no experience more satisfies childhood dreams than being part of an Australian cricket tour of England. Yet by August, three months into the tour, I was as low as I have ever been during my cricket life.

This decline began during the first Test, at Edgbaston. But even though we lost this game, and personally there was little for me to cheer about as far as my batting and bowling went, I can still appreciate it as a great Test match. We stuffed it up on the first morning, but after that we played pretty well. Trouble was, England was fantastic at the start, and performed admirably throughout. So for all but the first session, it was two teams, both playing good cricket, fighting for supremacy.

The pitch at the start was a real seamer, doing truckloads, and we were bowled out for only 118 despite the fact that there weren't too many awful shots played. It was simply a case of the deck doing plenty and the Poms, especially Andy Caddick and Darren Gough, bowling exceedingly well. Maybe we weren't quite switched on, and certainly had it not been for Shane Warne's belligerent 47 at the end we wouldn't have even reached three figures, but in my view it was one of those situations in which it was more appropriate to give credit to the bowlers rather than criticise the batsmen. I was dismissed by Devon Malcolm, who bowled really quick, caught by Mark Ealham in the slip cordon off a lifter aimed at my armpit. Sure enough, the whispers again turned to shouts that I couldn't handle the short ball. My view at the time was that, on that pitch, against high quality bowling, any batsman would struggle. After all, I was the seventh wicket to fall, for 48.

When we bowled, again I didn't think we did too much wrong, but after they struggled to 3–50, Nasser Hussain and Graham Thorpe were quite magnificent, adding 288 for the fourth wicket. Six wickets then fell for 140, which left us 360 behind as Mark Taylor and Matthew Elliott went out for our second innings.

Tubby, of course, was still in very average form and the general consensus was that if he failed here he would be axed. It had reached the point where his troubles were impacting on the mood of the side. Paul Reiffel, a late replacement on this tour, wrote in his autobiography that when he arrived in England to join the team, the mood of the squad was lower than anything he had experienced in his previous five years in the Australian side. Having been with the team since the start of the tour—and being someone who likes to keep to himself a fair bit anyway—I wasn't conscious of such deterioration in morale at the time, but thinking back now, it was there. However, no bad feeling was directed at Tubby, so when he came out and put together one of cricket's bravest hundreds the relief we felt was palpable. Even though we still lost the Test, the fact that we fought back, and that the revival was led by our skipper, meant that we took plenty of positives out of the game.

When we began our second innings, the Edgbaston pitch was still in excellent shape, though perhaps not quite as flat as it had been when Hussain and Thorpe had batted. It was beginning to crack, and maybe there was a hint of uneven bounce, so what Tubby—and Greg Blewett, who also scored a century—did was quite brilliant. They gave us an outside chance of victory, and if the rest of us had batted better we might even have won. When I came in, they started firing short ones at me; I made it to 24 before another short one got me out, caught in the slip cordon. I walked off fully aware that my opponents reckoned I couldn't play the short one, that most of the cricket world agreed with them, that many of my team-mates agreed with them. (In his *Ashes Diary*, Steve Waugh wrote, 'Michael Bevan again fell to the short ball, a fact that will be preying on his mind from now on. His struggles in this area must be sorted out quickly, or else they will be ruthlessly exposed.')

Something we stress in squad meetings is the fact that top-level cricket is about identifying fallabilities in opponents and exploiting them. The word was well and truly out across the cricket planet that I didn't have the technique to handle the short ball. But I'd always truly believed that my technique was OK; all the work I'd done in the nets over the previous three years had confirmed this. But I'd go out in the middle . . . and still get out to them. I didn't let things flow and thus was that critical split-second slow to react. I knew the short ball was coming, but I didn't have the clarity of mind to simply let my natural instincts take over. To relax.

Could I have fixed this? Yes I could have, but at this stage of my cricket life I still hadn't recognised what the problem was. I guess I thought every Test cricketer was as tight and apprehensive as I was, but that they camouflaged it better than I did. I never stopped to compare my mental state when I batted in the one-dayers to the way I approached the Tests. Instead, I decided that maybe the critics were right, that I needed even more maintenance on my technique, so back to the nets I went. And I still retained the fatalistic belief that everything would be all right in the end, that a big score was just around the corner. I can clearly remember sitting in the dressing room after getting out, thinking, 'Why is this happening to me?' I pictured myself weathering the barrage of short stuff, and then blazing away to a big hundred. In my dreams. I know now that such was my fractured mental approach, I was never going to make that big score. But I also know

now, with due modesty, that if I could have relaxed and got my mental approach right, I was technically good enough to score plenty of Test-match runs. Still am.

We lost our last nine wickets for 150 runs, our last seven for 84, which left England just 118 to win. Mike Atherton and Alec Stewart then came out and smashed us, to complete what appeared on the surface to be a clear victory. It wasn't quite that.

While I'm a reserved type of person, the opposite could be said of my English wife Tracy. One of the questions everybody asks her is, 'Who do you support, England or Australia?' Her reply is always the same—she supports me.

During the first Test, as England continued to pile up the runs, a few of us out on the field noticed a fair bit of commotion coming from one of the grandstands. The local fans were chanting 'The Ashes are coming home!' at every opportunity. Everywhere in the crowd, it seemed, there were banners proclaiming the same thing. It really was a charged atmosphere.

Suddenly, through this sea of English parochialism, a solitary Australian flag appeared, being carried from one end of the grandstand to the other. It wasn't until the third crossing that we noticed the ringleader of this little escapade was about five foot six, blonde, and looked remarkably similar to the wife of a left-handed, middle-order batsman in the Australian team. This certainly lightened the mood among the lads, and I realised that I'd definitely picked the right partner to spend my life with.

First game after the Test, against Nottinghamshire, I made 75 not out in our only innings, and then made 11 and 13 against Leicestershire. There was never a question of my being left out of the second Test, but when I went out to bat, I truly did feel like a prisoner on his way to his execution. I'd even lost the inclination to guts it out. Basically, I was shot. I think everyone who saw me batting in the second and third Tests of this series realised that. It was probably the worst time in my cricket life. However, by the end of the tour, even though I hardly contributed at all—runs- and wickets-wise—after I was dropped following the third Test, I'd reached a peace with myself. I knew what I needed to do.

Same as in 1994–95, the guy who took my spot in the Test team—this time Ricky Ponting—immediately scored a brilliant century. For a while, I was bitter, until I sat down and said to myself, 'I'm never going to play Test cricket again unless something changes'. What to change? I sat down and spoke with my wife for hours and hours, analysing my cricket career to date, and by the time we'd finished, I'd come up with the solution, or at least what I hoped was the solution. I finally acknowledged that my mental state when I went to bat wasn't right; it was the first time that I've ever said that in my life. But as soon as I said it, and meant it, it was like a huge weight had been lifted from me.

I stood up to myself, for myself. I resolved to turn negatives into positives, to go out to bat expecting to succeed rather than waiting to fail, to enjoy the pressure and responsibility rather than be suffocated by it. If my preparation was perfect, then I was good enough to do all of this, so long as I didn't let outside influences fog my thinking. I knew that if I didn't change my thinking in this way, I would never reach my goal of being an accomplished Test cricketer. And I wanted to play a lot more Test cricket. By the end of that tour, I'd actually started hitting the ball well again, only this time I knew why I was hitting it well again. My last game was against Kent at Canterbury and I scored 55 and 47 not out and batted really well. So I left England on a good note, on a happy note, even though it was probably the worst tour of my life.

It's frustrating for me now to know that at times through my Test career my mental set-up wasn't right. Equally frustrating is the fact that my weakness was not something that stifled me every time I went out to bat, but only when I went out to bat in some Test matches when I felt the weight of expectations—from myself and others—most keenly. My focus wasn't always clear enough to withstand these pressures, because I wasn't perceptive enough to identify them—until my reputation as a Test batsman was pretty tarnished.

Most frustrating is the fact that I strongly believe that I have worked out what I need to do to achieve success at the highest level, that I know that I am a much better player today than I was way back then, but that I might never play Test cricket for Australia again. But in keeping with my policy of turning negatives into positives, I haven't stopped too much to dwell on this fact; rather, I've concentrated on enjoying my cricket, whomever I might be playing for. I'm going to finish up my career on a happy note. I love playing for NSW, have enjoyed playing county cricket; most of all, I love playing one-day cricket for Australia and have approached every one-dayer as deliberately and thoroughly as I ever would a Test match. Whether other players involved in both forms of the international game ease off just a fraction in the one-dayers, I do not know, but over the last five years they have been my Test matches and I most certainly have never held back at all. I have never lost that pure, simple desire to play for Australia. And I'm enjoying my cricket now far more than I did in England in 1997.

AUSTRALIA V ENGLAND, FIRST TEST, 1997
EDGBASTON, BIRMINGHAM
5-8 JUNE 1997
TOSS: AUSTRALIA

Australia first innings

*MA Taylor c Butcher b Malcolm		7
MTG Elliott b Gough		6
GS Blewett c Hussain b Gough		7
ME Waugh b Gough		5
SR Waugh c Stewart b Caddick		12
MG Bevan c Ealham b Malcolm		8
+IA Healy c Stewart b Caddick		0
JN Gillespie lbw Caddick		4
SK Warne c Malcolm b Caddick		47
MS Kasprowicz c Butcher b Caddick		17
GD McGrath not out		1
Extras (w 2, nb 2)		4
Total (all out, 31.5 overs)		118

FW: 1-11 (Elliott), 2-15 (Taylor), 3-26 (ME Waugh), 4-28 (Blewett), 5-48 (SR Waugh), 6-48 (Healy), 7-48 (Bevan), 8-54 (Gillespie), 9-110 (Kasprowicz), 10-118 (Warne)
Bowling: Gough 10-1-43-3, Malcolm 10-2-25-2, Caddick 11.5-1-50-5

England first innings

MA Butcher c Healy b Kasprowicz		8
*MA Atherton c Healy b McGrath		2
+AJ Stewart c Elliott b Gillespie		18
N Hussain c Healy b Warne		207
GP Thorpe c Bevan b McGrath		138
JP Crawley c Healy b Kasprowicz		1
MA Ealham not out		53
RDB Croft c Healy b Kasprowicz		24
D Gough c Healy b Kasprowicz		0
AR Caddick lbw Bevan		0
Extras (b 4, lb 7, w 1, nb 15)		27
Total (9 wickets declared, 138.4 overs)		478

DNB: DE Malcolm
FW: 1-8 (Atherton), 2-16 (Butcher), 3-50 (Stewart), 4-338 (Thorpe), 5-345 (Crawley), 6-416 (Hussain), 7-460 (Croft), 8-463 (Gough), 9-478 (Caddick)
Bowling: McGrath 32-8-107-2, Kasprowicz 39-8-113-4, Gillespie 10-1-48-1, Warne 35-8-110-1, Bevan 10.4-0-44-1, SR Waugh 12-2-45-0

Australia second innings

MTG Elliott b Croft	66
*MA Taylor c & b Croft	129
GS Blewett c Butcher b Croft	125
SR Waugh lbw Gough	33
MG Bevan c Hussain b Gough	24
ME Waugh c Stewart b Gough	1
+IA Healy c Atherton b Ealham	30
SK Warne c & b Ealham	32
MS Kasprowicz c Butcher b Ealham	0
JN Gillespie run out	0
GD McGrath not out	0
Extras (b 18, lb 12, w 2, nb 5)	37
Total (all out, 144.4 overs)	477

FW: 1-133 (Elliott), 2-327 (Taylor), 3-354 (Blewett), 4-393 (Bevan), 5-399 (ME Waugh), 6-431 (SR Waugh), 7-465 (Healy), 8-465 (Kasprowicz), 9-477 (Gillespie), 10-477 (Warne).
Bowling: Gough 35-7-123-3, Malcolm 21-6-52-0; Croft 43-10-125-3, Caddick 30-6-87-0, Ealham 15.4-3-60-3

England second innings

MA Butcher lbw Kasprowicz	14
*MA Atherton not out	57
+AJ Stewart not out	40
Extras (b 4, lb 4)	8
Total (1 wicket, 21.3 overs)	119

FW: 1-29 (Butcher)
Bowling: McGrath 7-1-42-0, Kasprowicz 7-0-42-1, Warne 7.3-0-27-0

Close of play

Day 1: England 3-200 (Hussain 80*, Thorpe 83*)
Day 2: England 6-449 (Ealham 32*, Croft 18*)
Day 3: Australia 1-256 (Taylor 108*, Blewett 61*)

RESULT: ENGLAND WON BY NINE WICKETS
UMPIRES: SA BUCKNOR (WI) AND P WILLEY
MAN OF THE MATCH: N HUSSAIN

GAME 15

AUSTRALIA V SOUTH AFRICA
SECOND TEST
SYDNEY
2–5 JANUARY 1998

This was a historic Test for Australia. It was Steve Waugh's 100th Test, making him the third Australian after Allan Border and David Boon to reach the milestone. On the final day, Shane Warne knocked over Jacques Kallis, his 300th Test wicket, becoming the second Australian, after DK Lillee, to take that many. He'd been playing Test cricket for exactly six years. It was also, quite possibly, my last Test match. As I write this, I have never played another, and the prospects of a recall diminish by the day.

When Warney was originally selected in the Test team, his accuracy was quite phenomenal for such an inexperienced leggie. Facing him in a Shield match around this time, he would bowl 15 overs and not bowl a bad ball. And all the time, he was putting such a buzz on the ball that he was getting a beautiful loop, drift and turn. Up until he hurt his shoulder in 1998 it was the same. What do you do against a bowler who turns it as much as he does and never gives you a bad ball? Against a craftsman who is so smart and adept that he knows exactly what he needs to do against every batsman he confronts, is confident enough to try it, and skilful enough to do it? Awesome is my word for him; some days he's nearly impossible to bat against. Since 1998, maybe he hasn't put quite the same spin on the ball—not consistently anyway—but he's still one helluva bowler.

Shane's wrong 'un doesn't turn as much as many other wrist-spinners. Dare I say, it doesn't spin as much as mine. This, I believe, is a result of the way he bowls, not quite right over the top, which sure gives him every chance to rip a leg-break and whip through his amazing flipper, but makes it difficult to get the back of the hand facing down the pitch and the fingers pointing up into the sky, which you need to do if you want the googly to turn sharply. When I bowl, my arm is close to right-next-to-the-ear perpendicular, which makes it harder for me to really turn the leggie—instead it tends to skid through—but does give me a chance to make the wrong 'un bite.

Having said this, I have no doubt that if Shane wanted to bowl a world-class googly he could do so. He probably doesn't use it that much because he doesn't think he needs to. I've got to bowl mine often because it's my most dangerous delivery. Same with the Pakistani leggie Mushtaq Ahmed, who would never die wondering if the wrong 'un was the right option.

Warney's bowler-keeper partnership with Ian Healy was one of the joys of cricket in the 1990s, the thing that established Heals' reputation as one of the finest wicketkeepers of all time. What confidence it must have given Shane to know that whatever he bowled, Heals would do the right thing by it, whether it be taking a thin *or* thick edge or preventing a rare errant delivery sneaking through for byes. Heals had a real presence behind the stumps, which added to the relentless pressure Shane put on the batsmen.

Heals has said that I was tougher to keep to than Warney, which simply reflects the fact that Shane was accurate while I, most often, was not. I also generated more bounce than Shane, and was quicker through the air. Still, Heals was never short of superb when keeping to me. Our greatest moment as a pair came at Old Trafford in the third Ashes Test of 1997, when the left-handed Mark Butcher was stumped after I speared one down outside Butcher's pads. It pitched on the batsman's popping crease, after Butcher tried to turn it on the legside, missed it, and stumbled forward. Heals' positioning was perfect; he may have been unsighted but his gloves were down low, not worrying if the ball spat off the crease or footmarks, waiting for it to come through. And after the ball entered his gloves, he had the bails off in a flash. It was all his magical work; I was hardly entitled to claim the dismissal.

The other two blokes who were brilliant in this match at Old Trafford were Mark Taylor and Steve Waugh. When we saw the pitch before the Test we all thought it was a seamer on which any captain who won the toss would bowl first. In fact, many of us wondered whether the track might even have been doctored, whether the home authorities might have been so worried about Warney that they'd left as much grass on the wicket as they dared, and a bit of moisture, too. Remember, two Tests earlier at Edgbaston we'd been overwhelmed, for not much more than a hundred, by Darren Gough and Andy Caddick. So you can imagine our surprise when Tubby announced that he had won the toss and we were BATTING! It was one of those situations where none of us wanted to actually say we thought our captain was crazy but I'm sure a few of us were thinking that way. However, he was right and we were all wrong. By day two, the pitch had dried out into a real turner and Warney was able to spin his magic.

Of course, a captain is only as good as his players, and on the first day Steve Waugh scored a century and batted wonderfully in conditions that proved too difficult for the rest of us. This was a knock that demonstrated what a rare talent Tugga is, technically superb and with an ability to concentrate that I imagine few in the history of the game have been able to match. I admired the way he put the pitch conditions out of his mind-set, and focused on the job at hand, which involved surviving the awkward deliveries and taking as many runs as possible from the loose ones.

Unfortunately I wasn't much help to Steve, making 7 in the first innings and a duck in the second (when Steve made 116, becoming the first right-handed Australian to ever score a hundred in each innings of an Ashes Test). In the short time I was in the middle, I was peppered with short stuff; mentally I'd lost the fight, so I succumbed rather meekly. I hadn't bowled that well either, and as the team celebrated a crucial victory, I resigned myself to being left out for the next Test.

It's interesting, looking at the way the following Australian season went for these four guys—Taylor, Waugh, Healy and Warne—and for me, too. I would play only one more full-scale international, Test or one-dayer, with Tubby and Heals, and that would be the 1998 New Year's Test against South Africa in Sydney. Both guys had been left out of the Australian one-day team, as the selectors went full-steam ahead with the new policy of choosing two separate teams. Stephen was now captain of the one-day team, and he began somewhat rockily, as the players, fans and media took time to get used to this two-captain/two-team arrangement. Warney, meanwhile, had a terrific summer, the feature of which was his bowling in the Tests. He took 39 wickets, including 11 at the SCG when I was selected—a bit out of the blue as I remember—in that same role I'd filled with some success the previous year: the second spinner, batting at seven.

I can't remember walking out to the middle for that innings thinking that my entire future in Test cricket was on the line, though with hindsight it probably was. I'm sure I would have known that a big innings was essential, but my attitude had changed and I had been determined all season to enjoy myself and simply take whatever came my way. In the Shield to that point I'd scored 409 runs at 102.25, including two hundreds, and I'd also made 102 runs at 34 in the four one-day internationals we'd played to that point in the season, so I felt I was in good nick. But I made only 12 in Sydney, caught at slip off a ball from the tall feisty off-spinner Pat Symcox that spun and bounced. It was a good delivery, and a bit ironic that I fell to a spinner after I'd batted pretty well against Allan Donald, who didn't mind banging them in.

The press cuttings of this game reflect the fact that I handled the quicks all right. 'Donald did not pitch the right length to Bevan, dropping too short,' wrote Peter Roebuck. 'Alas, Bevan's promising innings was cut short by spin . . .'

'Bevan carried himself with assurance,' commented Malcolm Knox in the *Sydney Morning Herald*, 'and it was a surprise when he gloved a kicking ball to the slip cordon . . .'

I bowled OK in the first innings, too, but not so well in the only three overs I sent down in the second, and that was that. They went with two spinners for the next Test in Adelaide, but Warney's support guy was Stuart MacGill, not me, with Heals moving up to No. 7. Those three overs in the second innings might have only gone for 18 runs, but, looking back, I reckon they were very expensive—they may have cost me my Test place, at least for one more game. In the selectors' eyes at least, I was now a one-day batsman.

AUSTRALIA V SOUTH AFRICA, SECOND TEST, 1997–98
SYDNEY CRICKET GROUND
2–5 JANUARY 1998
TOSS: SOUTH AFRICA

South Africa first innings

AM Bacher lbw Blewett	39
G Kirsten c Taylor b McGrath	11
JH Kallis run out	16
*WJ Cronje c Taylor b Warne	88
HH Gibbs c Healy b Bevan	54
BM McMillan c Elliott b Bevan	6
SM Pollock c Taylor b Warne	18
+DJ Richardson b Warne	6
PL Symcox c Healy b Warne	29
AA Donald not out	4
PR Adams c SR Waugh b Warne	0
Extras (b 4, lb 4, w 1, nb 7)	16
Total (all out, 124.1 overs)	287

Fall: 1-25 (Kirsten), 2-70 (Bacher), 3-70 (Kallis), 4-167 (Gibbs), 5-174 (McMillan), 6-228 (Pollock), 7-236 (Richardson), 8-276 (Cronje), 9-287 (Symcox), 10-287 (Adams)
Bowling: McGrath 20-6-51-1, Reiffel 24-7-48-0, Warne 32.1-8-75-5, Bevan 23-3-56-2, Blewett 13-5-30-1, SR Waugh 8-4-10-0, ME Waugh 3-1-5-0, Elliott 1-0-4-0

Australia first innings

MTG Elliott c McMillan b Symcox	32
*MA Taylor c Richardson b Pollock	11
GS Blewett b McMillan	28
ME Waugh lbw Pollock	100
SR Waugh b Donald	85
RT Ponting c & b Adams	62
MG Bevan c McMillan b Symcox	12
+IA Healy not out	46
PR Reiffel b Donald	0
SK Warne lbw Pollock	12
GD McGrath c Richardson b Donald	14
Extras (b 1, lb 12, nb 6)	19
Total (all out, 167.4 overs)	421

Fall: 1-35 (Taylor), 2-59 (Elliott), 3-103 (Blewett), 4-219 (ME Waugh), 5-317 (SR Waugh), 6-337 (Bevan), 7-354 (Ponting), 8-357 (Reiffel), 9-385 (Warne), 10-421 (McGrath)
Bowling: Donald 30.4-5-81-3, Pollock 33-8-71-3, Symcox 39-11-103-2, Adams 38-9-66-1, McMillan 18-5-55-1, Kallis 8-1-30-0, Cronje 1-0-2-0

South Africa second innings

G Kirsten lbw McGrath	0
AM Bacher c Ponting b Reiffel	2
JH Kallis b Warne	45
*WJ Cronje c Ponting b Warne	5
HH Gibbs c Blewett b Warne	1
BM McMillan b Warne	11
SM Pollock c Taylor b Warne	4
+DJ Richardson c & b Warne	0
PL Symcox b Reiffel	38
AA Donald c Healy b Reiffel	2
PR Adams not out	1
Extras (b 2, lb 1, nb 1)	4
Total (all out, 53.0 overs)	113

Fall: 1-1 (Kirsten), 2-3 (Bacher), 3-21 (Cronje), 4-27 (Gibbs), 5-41 (McMillan), 6-55 (Pollock), 7-55 (Richardson), 8-96 (Kallis), 9-112 (Symcox), 10-113 (Donald)
Bowling: Reiffel 12-3-14-3, McGrath 5-2-8-1, Warne 21-9-34-6, Blewett 2-1-1-0, Bevan 3-0-18-0, ME Waugh 10-2-35-0

Close of play:
Day 1: South Africa 5-197 (Cronje 56*, Pollock 1*)
Day 2: Australia 3-174 (ME Waugh 78*, SR Waugh 18*)
Day 3: Australia 9-392 (Healy 31*, McGrath 3*)

RESULT: AUSTRALIA WON BY AN INNINGS AND 21 RUNS
UMPIRES: DB HAIR AND P WILLEY (ENG)
MAN OF THE MATCH: SK WARNE

GAME 16

This was a strange tournament, and as much as I remember the cricket, I remember even more the heat in which we had to play some of the matches. You can't perform at your best in 45° heat (as it was in Ahmedabad and seemed to be in Kochi as well), and you can't prepare for such oppressive conditions either; if you tried to, you'd kill yourself in the process.

I recall very vividly the heat in Kochi, the 97 per cent humidity and, most of all, the stomach bug I caught two days before the game. I went into that match totally dehydrated and having eaten nothing for 48 hours. And yet, after I scored 65 from 82 balls, my gear was worse than saturated. Where the sweat came from I have no idea, but afterwards I felt totally wiped out. I only hit two fours in that innings, and could hardly run at all between the wickets by the end of it.

One of the doctrines always preached in the Australian dressing room is to run as hard as you possibly can between wickets. Every run counts. But in that steamy environment you can blow out too early if you don't pace yourself. Until I played in such torrid conditions, I could never understand why a batsman such as the former Sri Lankan captain Arjuna Ranatunga would rarely run hard between the wickets. Then I realised that he was probably just reflecting the circumstances in which he played most of his cricket; if you end up batting for any length of time, it's so hard over there to maintain your concentration if you're constantly fighting fatigue and dizziness. The fact we are required to play in such conditions is a reason why so much emphasis is placed on fitness these days.

We lost our round two matches against India, but beat Zimbabwe twice, which was enough to get us into the final of this tri-nation competition. Once into that decider, we weren't so much looking for revenge as simply wanting to play some good cricket against a team that had had much the better of the two Australian teams—Test and one-day—for most of the time since the Test tour had begun nearly two months before.

The Delhi wicket on which the final was played looked to be what we'd expected—flat, slow and low. India's captain Mohammad Azharuddin won the toss and batted, and first ball of his sixth over, Damien Fleming very unexpectedly produced a real flyer to Sachin Tendulkar. It could nearly have been called wide, as it bounced up near shoulder height, clipped his glove and went through to the keeper. Tendulkar had belted us in the preliminary matches, and now we had him out for 15. Soon, the wicket settled down; in fact, it was never too lively bar that one delivery, for which Flemo deserves all the credit, and we restricted India to 227.

I batted 4, in at 2–56 after Mark Waugh and Ricky Ponting had added 50 for the second wicket in 10 overs. By making a quick start, they really set it up for me to bat the way I wanted to. I thought, let's get us home; that's all I thought about. It was one of those innings where I just made sure we won. I probably could have done more and taken more of a chance, but I felt I chose the right option. After Punter was dismissed to make it 3–84, Stephen sent Warney in as a pinch hitter to bump up the run-rate, and he scored 14 at a run a ball, after which the captain came out himself and smashed a superb 57 from 54 deliveries. On that pitch, which by late afternoon was very slow and low, that was quite an effort. He played the whacking role magnificently.

Maybe sometimes I have a tendency to bat to the situation, rather than bat to my capabilities. I probably could have been more aggressive, but I was happy to measure how my team-mates were going, work out what I needed to do to get us home, and focus on that. We eventually won with eight balls to spare, and I finished 75 not out, scored off 127 deliveries. After Stephen was dismissed, Tom Moody was able to come out and score four runs from 13 deliveries, to underline the fact that we'd timed our run-chase pretty well.

I sometimes find that wanting to be there at the end can become so ingrained in my mind that worrying about scoring quickly and hitting every bad ball for four is no longer an issue. What matters is simply keeping the required run-rate happening, and keeping my wicket intact. I have never batted in a manner in which I've put too much pressure on my batting partners; if we need eight an over, then I try to time my run-scoring so we'll hit that eight an over and I'll be there in the end. If we need four an over, then I'll bat according to that requirement and I'll be there at the end. This means, of course, that we don't always achieve victory with as many overs to spare as we could. However, more times than not, we've achieved that victory.

This was the first Australian tour where the one-day squad was distinctly separate from the Test team. If there had been any birth pains with this concept, they'd been alleviated by the time we arrived in India; though there had definitely been controversy over the move when it was first introduced, mainly because we weren't immediately in sparkling form, and also because Stephen struggled with the bat a little in his early games as one-day captain. A critical moment had come earlier in 1998, in the first final of the Carlton & United Series at the MCG against South Africa, when Tugga pushed Adam Gilchrist up to open and Gilly—who had, it must be remembered, replaced an icon in Heals—responded so positively to the responsibility. First up, he only scored 20 from 27 balls, but looked at home at the top of the order. Then, three days later in Sydney, he belted a glorious even hundred from 104 balls, we won easily, and Gilly has been opening for Australia in one-day internationals ever since. From that game on, the criticism of the two-team concept began to die away.

I can remember when Adam Gilchrist first came into the NSW team in the early 1990s, he played purely as a batsman and couldn't score a run. How things have changed! He was always a very talented player, but I don't think anyone, even Gilly himself, could have believed that things would turn out the way they have. With Phil Emery locked into the NSW keeper role, a move to Western Australia gave Gilly the chance to play Shield cricket regularly as a keeper-batsman, and set him up to be—by 1997—pretty much universally accepted as second choice behind Ian Healy. Even by this stage, his batting had him on the edge of selection in the one-day team purely as a run-scorer, and precipitated one of the more controversial selection decisions of recent years: to sack Heals as the one-day keeper. I reckon Heals was very unlucky to lose that job at that time. He was still in excellent form, a magnificent keeper quite capable of contributing with the bat from the No. 7 or No. 8 spot, but Gilly brought even more to the team, and more so when Steve made that move to promote him to the top of the order.

I don't think there is any great secret to Gilly as a batsman. He's just supremely talented, plus he's a sensible, clear thinker who doesn't put any pressure on himself. He goes out and plays his shots, and he's very, very good at playing those shots. He's a fantastic cross-bat player, maybe as good as I've seen, with an ability to improvise at the right time. There are quite a few guys who can play unconventional shots— the reverse sweep, the help-it-on-its-way over the keeper or first slip, the swinging the good-length ball away forward of square leg—but Gilly has a rare, almost unique, ability to pick his moment. I believe Gilly is a very instinctive player—others who might try to bat his way would be playing with many risks. His record and consistency show that it is completely natural for him to play the way he does.

As a Test batsman, coming in at No. 7, Gilly has made a habit of reserving his best for the tough times, when Australia really needs him. That's an uncanny ability. In my view, he's been the most productive of

Australia's Test batsmen in the last couple of years—as the wicketkeeper, batting seven—which is no mean feat considering the quality of players above him in the batting order. And when he changes the mood of a game, he does so very quickly, catching the other team off guard. Before they know it, the game is gone.

It must be frustrating for the disciples of the coaching manual seeing Gilly bat, watching him succeed while batting unconventionally. 'Always play straight' we were told when we were kids, well-meaning things like that, stock-standard advice. Often the conventional way is right, but not always. The way Gilly approaches his batting proves that. Everyone is different, we all have a natural way of playing, and it's important we never lose that. The fundamentals are important, and you can't survive without them—note that even when he's swinging away Gilly is always technically very sound, his eye is always on the ball and his balance is perfect—but they need to work with individual flair and character, otherwise the game becomes boring and opportunities are lost.

I know some people are still not convinced that having two separate Australian squads is the way to go, but I think the fact that across the cricket world, international teams are using different styles of players in their two teams strongly suggests that the move was, and is, right. I have come to appreciate that some players are better suited to one form of the game than the other, while remaining convinced in my own mind that this is not necessarily the case with me.

One thing that happened in the past was that players were often selected to play one-day internationals on the back of their form in Test cricket or the Sheffield Shield, while some players who had performed well in domestic one-day cricket weren't getting a look in. As players who were strong in the longer version of the game were being selected automatically, inevitably some of the skills needed to play excellent one-day cricket weren't being utilised. This has now changed to a large extent, and will continue to change over time.

AUSTRALIA V INDIA, PEPSI TRIANGULAR CUP FINAL, 1997–98
FEROZ SHAH KOTLA, DELHI
14 APRIL 1998 (50-OVERS MATCH)
TOSS: INDIA

India innings

SC Ganguly c Gilchrist b Moody	29
SR Tendulkar c Gilchrist b Fleming	15
*M Azharuddin c Bevan b SR Waugh	44
NS Sidhu c Fleming b SR Waugh	38
A Jadeja c & b Kasprowicz	48
HH Kanitkar b Fleming	18
AB Agarkar c SR Waugh b Warne	4
+NR Mongia c Bevan b Fleming	14
A Kumble not out	1
BKV Prasad b Kasprowicz	1
RL Sanghvi run out	0
Extras (b 2, lb 6, w 6, nb 1)	15
Total (all out, 49.3 overs)	227

Fall: 1-37 (Tendulkar), 2-58 (Ganguly), 3-128 (Azharuddin), 4-144 (Sidhu), 5-177 (Kanitkar), 6-185 (Agarkar), 7-218 (Jadeja), 8-225 (Mongia), 9-227 (Prasad), 10-227 (Sanghvi)
Bowling: Fleming 10-1-47-3, Kasprowicz 9.3-0-43-2, Moody 10-0-40-1, Warne 10-0-35-1, SR Waugh 7-0-42-2, Lehmann 3-0-12-0

Australia innings

ME Waugh b Kumble	20
+AC Gilchrist c Tendulkar b Agarkar	1
RT Ponting st Mongia b Sanghvi	41
MG Bevan not out	75
SK Warne b Prasad	14
*SR Waugh b Kumble	57
TM Moody c Jadeja b Agarkar	4
DS Lehmann not out	6
Extras (lb 6, w 5, nb 2)	13
Total (6 wickets, 48.4 overs)	231

DNB: DR Martyn, DW Fleming, MS Kasprowicz
Fall: 1-6 (Gilchrist), 2-56 (ME Waugh), 3-84 (Ponting), 4-111 (Warne), 5-210 (SR Waugh), 6-219 (Moody)
Bowling: Prasad 7-0-43-1, Agarkar 10-1-53-2, Kumble 9.4-2-36-2, Kanitkar 7-0-35-0, Sanghvi 10-0-45-1, Tendulkar 5-0-13-0

RESULT: AUSTRALIA WON BY FOUR WICKETS
UMPIRES: V CHOPRA AND VK RAMASWAMY
MAN OF THE MATCH: SR WAUGH

GAME 17

**AUSTRALIA V INDIA
COCA-COLA CUP FINAL
SHARJAH
24 APRIL 1998**

Sachin Tendulkar had scored a heap of runs against us in the Pepsi Triangular one-day series in India, and then we had to bowl at him again in Sharjah less than two weeks later. In India, we'd lost all our preliminary matches but then prevailed against India in the final; in Sharjah the roles were reversed. This time, we went into the final undefeated, but the mighty Sachin was too good for us in the decider. Afterwards, our captain Steve Waugh, ranking the little maestro in terms of the greatest batsmen in history, remarked, 'You take Bradman away, and he is next up, I reckon'. I don't pretend to know as much about cricket history as Tugga does, but I can't imagine anyone—bar a bloke who was able to average 100 every time he went to bat—being better than Sachin.

'We couldn't do much more,' Steve continued, reflecting on Tendulkar's century in the Sharjah final. 'He almost won the game for them single-handedly.'

I wasn't sure what Steve meant when he said 'almost'!

Before that competition decider, we faced India in the sixth and last

THE BEST OF BEVAN 117

game of the preliminaries of the competition, in an intriguing situation where we needed to win to make the final while India only needed to avoid a heavy defeat. However, after we made 7–284 from our 50 overs, of which I scored 101, that big loss was a distinct possibility for India. And remained a distinct possibility even when an extraordinary sandstorm blew in from the desert, diminishing visibility to less than zero and making play impossible, and reducing our opponent's winning objective to 276 from 46 overs. To make the final they required 237. And Sachin smashed 143, from 131 deliveries, including nine fours and five sixes, not being dismissed until his team had passed that 237 run target.

The stadium was packed with, I'd guess, around 25 000 spectators, all of them Indian supporters, or, to be more precise, Sachin devotees. Now, I didn't mind the fact that everyone was backing our opponent, but I was a little concerned that the capacity of the joint was more like 20 000. Everyone was in good humour, especially as their hero tore us to shreds, but it was one of those situations where, no matter how far from the boundary I was fielding, it felt as if the patrons were breathing down my neck.

Still, we won that match, and to be honest we weren't too concerned about having to try to contain the little maestro again in the final. After all, there was no way he could bat that well again. And he didn't. He batted better.

The reason I've spotlighted these Sharjah matches for this book is twofold. One, I wanted to write briefly about Sachin, about what makes him *so* good. And two, I wanted to write briefly about the evolution of the one-day game, because it was around this time—the first half of 1998—that most people in the cricket world came to accept that it wasn't automatically the case that your Test team was also your best one-day team.

First, a few words on Sachin. As a one-day batsman, he possesses every shot you can possibly think of. There's no weakness. The closest thing I can think of to a vulnerability is that maybe, sometimes, he tries to dictate at *every* opportunity in the first 10 or 15 overs, which occasionally leads to his downfall. However, in those situations, if he does survive that period, he goes on to a classic innings, one of his very best. And when he does that, India usually wins.

His footwork and balance are magnificent. That's obvious, and to be honest I'm not sure if he is any better in this regard than a few other exceptional batsmen in the game today. What sets him apart, in my view, is his confidence and focus. When he dons the pads he suddenly becomes almost arrogant—not in his manner, but in the way he seems to automatically move into the right position for every delivery. When he bats, he has a counter for any situation he might find himself in, and he knows it, which makes him extremely hard to bowl to, and extremely hard to devise game plans for. Part of this, I'm sure, comes back to his understanding of the game and also to the fact that he prepares himself so well, but another part of it is an inherent gift that no other player today has. He's special. He belongs on a different page in the cricket book to the rest of us.

One interesting aspect to Sachin's career is that he didn't open the batting for India in one-day cricket until 1994, five years after he started in international cricket. In those first five years, as a middle-order batsman, he didn't score a single one-day international century. Since then, as an opener, he's hit more than 30 one-day hundreds at the highest level. Which got me thinking: how would I go as an opening bat in one-day cricket? The answer, I reckon, is that my average would be less, but my strike-rate would be higher. Now I know at first glance this might sound wrong, given that often as a middle-order batsman I bat in the helter-skelter of the final overs, but let me explain.

First, remember that my strategy is to bat to the situation; if we need four an over then I will try to score my runs at four an over. I'm not into slogging for the sake of it. At the same time, in the modern era of one-day cricket, an opening batsman needs to be proactive, to score at a good pace, to play shots that involve risks. Adam Gilchrist plays this role perfectly, as, of course, does Sachin Tendulkar. For these great openers, it's not so much a case of batting to a prescribed run-rate as a case of getting the team's innings off to a quickfire start.

The guys in the middle of the order make their runs in a different way. We have specific targets to meet, according to the match situation. You can keep the run-rate moving simply by consistently putting the ball into gaps for singles and twos in the middle order, but you can't do that in the first 15 overs, when the ball is new and hard and the bowlers are more aggressive. Early on, you've got to respect the excellent deliveries, and hit threes and fours off many of the good and mediocre ones. As an opener, I'd get more time at the crease to score bigger hundreds, but I'd also get out a lot more, as inevitably some of the risks I'd take to get the innings off to a quick start would bring me undone.

My admiration for Sachin Tendulkar is huge. I know how the weight of expectations can hinder your performance, and I'm proud of the way I've improved my ability to focus and take the pressure off myself. The pressure Sachin is under when he bats for India—and the way he absorbs it, seems to use it as a positive—is quite phenomenal. He gets a standing ovation every time he walks to the crease, gets stopped by every person who sees him on the street, to many he's a God. To score so well while receiving so much adulation, to worry only about his own goals, he must be very focused on what he's actually doing, never worrying about what everyone else is thinking about him or what expectations people have of him.

As an Australian cricketer in India, at times I find the constant attention almost suffocating. There's got to be a billion cricket fans in India, and there are times when it seems as if every single one of them is in the team hotel. They think nothing of giving you a call, popping up to your room, always after that elusive autograph. I should emphasise that it is not every Indian cricket fan who does this, but sometimes it feels as if it is. Sachin Tendulkar's situation must be 10 times, 100 times, 10 000 times more difficult. Never a spare moment. And today he's the greatest batsman in the world, maybe the second-best of all time. Amazing.

Back to Sharjah. Sachin beat us in the final, quite comfortably in the end, though he needed to be at his greatest to do so. After we made 9–272 from our 50 overs, he came out and made 134 from 131 deliveries. That meant he scored 277 off us, from 262 balls, in three days. The fans jammed into the ground were beside themselves with joy, as, I'm sure, were the millions more back home lapping it up as they watched on television. Our bowling attack was missing Glenn McGrath, but did include Shane Warne, Damien Fleming, Michael Kasprowicz, Tom Moody and the Waugh twins, so it wasn't bad. By the time he was out in the final, India needed just 25 more to win, from 33 balls, which they did with nine balls to spare.

These matches in Sharjah—the fact they really are a television product, and the fact they are played in a location with no real cricket tradition and no connection with Test cricket—reflected the period of transition, in terms of the way the cricket world sees its sport, that the game was going through. Today, one-day cricket is popular throughout the cricket world; Test cricket not to the same extent outside Australia. As this situation has evolved, some traditionalists have tried to denigrate limited-overs cricket, arguing that it is killing the game as we know it, but in my view there is plenty to like about the abbreviated game.

And I'm not saying this purely because it's where I make my living these days as an international cricketer. For one thing, one-day cricket gives players the opportunity to perform in front of huge crowds and colossal TV audiences. It's over in a day, you're guaranteed a result, astonishing skills and clever, flamboyant strokeplay are often on show. Some like to argue it can be boring, but show me a sport that is never that. The fact that bowlers are restricted to 10 overs is a negative, in that it restricts the opportunities for the great ones to strut their stuff, but there are still numerous examples of the best performers doing wonderful things in one-day matches. Think of Shane Warne at the 1999 World Cup. Batsmen from No. 4 down in the order have precious few chances to make really big scores, but when they do their efforts are special. It's not as huge a test of skills or concentration as Test cricket, but if you're smart enough to come up with an innovation that works you still get rewarded for it, sometimes rewarded grandly.

One of the big things about one-day cricket is the pressure. It's different to that of Test cricket in that whereas the pressure tends to come from the opposition being on the attack in Test matches, in the one-dayers it is the obligation to keep the scoreboard moving, to maximise your chances within the 50 overs, that causes the stress and divides the good players from the mediocre.

You also have to have flexibility in one-day cricket. You have to be able to play strokes. It's almost impossible to put yourself in a position to win a limited-overs match without taking chances. If you bat in the second 25 overs of a one-day innings, where I usually bat, your approach is dictated, to a large degree, by the field placements, the strategy of the bowlers, and the amount of runs per over you need to score.

And while critics like to tell everyone that one-day cricket is predictable, the fact is that different players have different ways of solving predicaments. For example, there are various ways to operate— even within the places in the batting order, from overs 1 to 15, 16 to 35 and 36 to 50—that can be effective. If you were to slide Adam Gilchrist down the batting order to No. 6 or No. 7, he'd do a great job I'm sure, and I'm equally sure that he wouldn't bat any differently from how he bats at the top of the innings. But the way he bats is very different from the way I bat, and I've gone all right doing it my way.

Every batsman has strengths and weaknesses, whether it be Test cricket or one-day cricket. In the one-dayers it makes sense for players to bat in positions that relate to their strengths, at a time in the innings when it is most likely they will contribute their best. Maybe rather than thinking of batsmen as being a No. 4 or No. 6 or No. 8, we should think of them as being a batsman for the 25th over, or the 35th over, or for as soon as the run-rate goes over a certain figure. Thus, for example, South Africa's great hitter Lance Klusener wouldn't bat at No. 7, he'd come in at the 30th over, whether his team is one down or six down. If his team is chasing a total, he'd be the next batsman in as soon as the run-rate went above six per over. Like every other strategy in one-day cricket you would need to be flexible; undoubtedly there would be times when it would be better for Jonty Rhodes or Jacques Kallis to go in ahead of Klusener, no matter what the match situation, but just as important is the fact that you don't want to waste Klusener's grand skills, or not use them at all.

From what I can gather, it probably took 25 years or more before the one-day game changed very much at all. Most of the international sides were basically Test teams in one-day clothing. The Australian team that won the 1987 World Cup was said to be innovative, but that was more in the way captain Allan Border and coach Bob Simpson used Test players to fill different roles. Steve Waugh's role as a bowler was much more critical in the shorter game. AB became a brilliant fieldsman at mid-wicket, a position he rarely filled in Test matches. Gradually, guys such as Simon O'Donnell, Peter Taylor and, at the end of his career, Dean Jones became key one-day players but fringe Test men, and established Test players such as Merv Hughes and occasionally Mark Taylor were left out of the one-dayers. It wasn't until the mid-1990s that the game really changed, when Sri Lanka won a World Cup using tactics far removed from the 'traditional' way, and shook up the cricket world. By then, established middle-order Test batsmen such as Sachin Tendulkar and Mark Waugh were opening the batting in one-day internationals; but if you look through the teams that played in the 1996 World Cup, you will see that most of them are very close to their Test XIs, maybe with an all-rounder or two instead of a specialist batsman or a specialist bowler.

Even in the last two or three years, we have seen some significant changes in how the game is played and exactly what is regarded as the ideal one-day cricketer. Such opinions will keep changing; I can see, at some stage down the track, there will be players who will be able to bat with both hands, throw with both hands, the reverse sweep will be a regulation shot. The next generation of young cricketers will grow up with skills we might not have dreamed of. And they'll be playing in locations even more unusual and bizarre than Sharjah. The only constant will be that you will have to be a good player to succeed. I reckon this will become more true than it has ever been.

AUSTRALIA V INDIA, COCA-COLA CUP FINAL, 1997–98
CA STADIUM, SHARJAH
24 APRIL 1998 (50-OVERS MATCH)
TOSS: INDIA

Australia innings

ME Waugh c Mongia b Agarkar	7
+AC Gilchrist c Mongia b Kanitkar	45
RT Ponting c Mongia b Prasad	1
TM Moody c Mongia b Agarkar	1
MG Bevan run out	45
*SR Waugh c Agarkar b Kanitkar	70
DS Lehmann c Sanghvi b Kumble	70
DR Martyn run out	16
SK Warne not out	6
MS Kasprowicz c Kanitkar b Prasad	0
DW Fleming not out	1
Extras (b 4, lb 3, w 2, nb 1)	10
Total (9 wickets, 50 overs)	272

Fall: 1-18 (ME Waugh), 2-19 (Ponting), 3-26 (Moody), 4-85 (Gilchrist), 5-121 (Bevan), 6-224 (SR Waugh), 7-255 (Lehmann), 8-263 (Martyn), 9-264 (Kasprowicz)
Bowling: Prasad 10-1-32-2, Agarkar 8-0-61-2, Kumble 10-1-46-1, Kanitkar 10-0-58-2, Sanghvi 10-0-45-0, Laxman 1-0-11-0, Tendulkar 1-0-12-0

India innings

SC Ganguly c Moody b Fleming	23
SR Tendulkar lbw Kasprowicz	134
+NR Mongia c Gilchrist b Fleming	28
*M Azharuddin c Gilchrist b Kasprowicz	58
A Jadeja not out	11
HH Kanitkar not out	6
Extras (b 1, lb 7, w 5, nb 2)	15
Total (4 wickets, 48.3 overs)	275

DNB: VVS Laxman, AB Agarkar, A Kumble, BKV Prasad, RL Sanghvi
Fall: 1-39 (Ganguly), 2-128 (Mongia), 3-248 (Tendulkar), 4-261 (Azharuddin)
Bowling: Fleming 10-1-47-2, Kasprowicz 10-0-48-2, Warne 10-0-61-0, Moody 9.3-0-63-0, ME Waugh 3-0-20-0, SR Waugh 6-0-28-0

RESULT: INDIA WON BY SIX WICKETS
UMPIRES: SA BUCKNOR (WI) AND JAVED AKHTAR (PAK)
MAN OF THE MATCH: SR TENDULKAR

GAME 18

AUSTRALIA V SOUTH AFRICA
COMMONWEALTH GAMES GOLD
MEDAL MATCH
KUALA LUMPUR
19 SEPTEMBER 1998

This was a new experience for us cricketers, being part of a large, multi-sport contingent such as the Australian Commonwealth Games team, and also being involved in a sport that was, at least as far as this event was concerned, a relatively minor one. Everything was different: we were playing international cricket in Malaysia, at an event that had never featured our sport before, staying in an 'athletes' village' rather than the five-star hotels we were accustomed to, marching in opening and closing ceremonies, playing for gold medals. And seeing how elite competitors from a variety of sports, most of them sports in which the individuals competed for themselves rather than as part of a team, prepared for one of the biggest events of their lives.

Our competition was a bit peculiar. The facilities were unlike anything I'd encountered in big-time cricket; almost quaint at times, and you never knew quite what to expect with the pitch conditions. Most of the wickets held up pretty well, though they turned a lot. The atmosphere was almost village cricket; small but enthusiastic groups of spectators close to the action generating as much atmosphere as they could. England didn't even show. India sent a team to Malaysia and another team to another one-day tournament being conducted at the same time in Toronto, Canada. The West Indies players represented their own island nations. I think it's fair to say that the teams didn't approach the task at hand with quite the same dedication as they might have approached a World Cup final, but it was still competitive.

When I was a kid, participating in track and field as well as cricket, I often dreamed of winning a Gold medal, usually at the Olympics, but when the Commonwealth Games were on, winning there became an ambition as well. So the fact that we missed out here, losing to South Africa in the Gold medal game, is a source of much disappointment. We'd cruised through the preliminaries, but slipped up in the game that mattered after being sent in by Shaun Pollock. Only Steve Waugh batted particularly well, as we crashed to 183 all out, and though we fought hard, there was rarely a moment in the South Africans' innings when it looked like we'd win.

I couldn't help coming to the conclusion, as I observed athletes from other sports, that even though cricketers have now reached a new high when it comes to 'professionalism' in our approach (and we're getting more and more professional every year), we still fail to match the levels of dedication required of athletes in other sports. I'm talking here purely in terms of the stress the athletes put on their minds and physiques during their preparation; the things they forego to have their bodies primed for the big day; the fact that months, even years of work are required for just one day, for that one big final; the fact that their training regimes can be so military, so lacking in variety; and the fact that compared to us cricketers, many don't get well paid. Our sacrifices are very different—we are required to spend huge slabs of time away from home and family, and because of our high profile our performances are constantly and heavily scrutinised by the media and the public, more so, on a continuing basis, than all but the very elite athletes in other Commonwealth Games sports.

Cricket-wise, the loss in the final was a timely reminder that you can't afford to take your foot off the pedal for even a minute against a team as good as the South Africans, or you pay the price. Elsewhere, I learnt plenty from watching other athletes in Kuala Lumpur. Some of the guys, most notably Gavin Robertson and Steve Waugh, spent a great deal of time communicating with other members of the Australian team, and they brought some of their observations back to team meetings. We also had a night where we invited the other members of the Australian contingent to a get-together, which was actually quite amusing because many of them were in awe of us while we were a little in awe of them. There was a perception among them that we were something of a 'Dream Team' who wouldn't react well to being required to bunk in the village, but that was far from the reality. We really appreciated the change and the spirit engendered by all the athletes mixing closely.

Shaun Pollock was the key figure in the final, taking the first four wickets to fall to a bowler in the match (I was run out for 13, the fourth wicket to fall; Shaun got the first three and the fifth). This was a bit ironic as the South Africans went into the game with three spinners, figuring that was the best way to contain us. Then their one front-line paceman came out and knocked us over. Shaun bowled beautifully, as he usually does, confirming again his reputation as one of the most feared all-rounders in the game.

In many ways Pollock's bowling is similar to our own Glenn McGrath's. Both of them have the ability to hit a 10 cent piece, right on a good length, continually. Batsmen facing Pollock are constantly thinking, 'What should I do? Should I take a chance, or see him out?' In my time with the Australian team, whenever we play South Africa, we devote a fair deal of time to determining how we're going to play Shaun Pollock. I should stress that we never forget that everyone has their own style, and is free to use that approach in whatever situation they might find themselves. But with Pollock, we're constantly discussing in team meetings the fact that he's a dangerous and intelligent hitter; and a bowler who's always hard to hit, someone who performs really well at the death when he usually bowls yorker length and is tough to get away. I've seen batsmen get really frustrated batting against him in a one-dayer. But never as frustrated, I must say, as I was the day he stood on the dais in Kuala Lumpur, gold medal around his neck, proudly singing his country's national anthem.

I'd have liked to have done that.

AUSTRALIA V SOUTH AFRICA, COMMONWEALTH GAMES GOLD MEDAL MATCH, 1998
PKNS CLUB, KUALA LUMPUR
19 SEPTEMBER 1998 (50-OVERS MATCH)
TOSS: SOUTH AFRICA

Australia innings

ME Waugh c Boucher b Pollock	2
+AC Gilchrist c Rindel b Pollock	15
RT Ponting c Dawson b Pollock	2
MG Bevan run out	13
*SR Waugh not out	90
DS Lehmann c Boucher b Pollock	26
TM Moody st Boucher b Adams	3
BE Young c Benkenstein b Adams	2
GR Robertson lbw Boje	2
MS Kasprowicz run out	12
DW Fleming run out	1
Extras (b 1, lb 2, w 11, nb 1)	15
Total (all out, 49.3 overs)	183

Fall: 1-10 (ME Waugh), 2-16 (Ponting), 3-28 (Gilchrist), 4-58 (Bevan), 5-121 (Lehmann), 6-124 (Moody), 7-142 (Young), 8-157 (Robertson), 9-177 (Kasprowicz), 10-183 (Fleming)
Bowling: Pollock 9-2-19-4, Kallis 6-1-21-0, Dawson 8.1-1-27-0, Crookes 10-0-43-0, Boje 8-0-36-1, Adams 8-0-33-2, Benkenstein 0.2-0-1-0

South Africa innings

AC Hudson c Bevan b Robertson	36
MJR Rindel c ME Waugh b Lehmann	67
DN Crookes c Moody b Robertson	3
JH Kallis c Gilchrist b Lehmann	44
HH Gibbs b Fleming	9
DM Benkenstein not out	2
*SM Pollock c Young b Lehmann	2
+MV Boucher not out	0
Extras (b 6, lb 1, w 10, nb 4)	21
Total (6 wickets, 46 overs)	184

DNB: N Boje, PR Adams, AC Dawson
Fall: 1-73 (Hudson), 2-86 (Crookes), 3-158 (Rindel), 4-172 (Gibbs), 5-181 (Kallis), 6-183 (Pollock)
Bowling: Fleming 10-1-44-1, Kasprowicz 5-0-34-0, Young 10-3-31-0, Robertson 10-2-28-2, Moody 4-0-15-0, Bevan 3-0-11-0, Lehmann 4-1-14-3

RESULT: SOUTH AFRICA WON BY FOUR WICKETS
UMPIRES: SA BUCKNOR AND KT FRANCIS

GAME 19

AUSTRALIA V ENGLAND
CARLTON & UNITED SERIES FIRST FINAL
SYDNEY
10 FEBRUARY 1999

With the amount of one-day cricket played every Australian summer, in the eyes of some observers one season can tend to blend into another. The cricket itself is invariably excellent and entertaining, hotly contested and more often than not sparked by a little controversy; yet if you ask many followers of the game when a particular memorable moment occurred, they'll look at you blankly and give a very general answer. Some like to point to this and use it as a criticism of the one-day game, as proof that the games are 'meaningless'. I don't agree. Yes, these responses do reflect the fact that we play a lot of limited-overs cricket, and, World Cup apart, the individual competitions are not regarded in many circles as being as prestigious as winning a Test series. What needs to happen is for the game—and by the 'game' I mean all the players, administrators, fans and media—to foster a sense of tradition for the one-day game, rather than sneer at it. The VB Series (as it was called in 2001–02), for example, has a history that goes back to 1979–80. But how often do we consider it? In contrast, during an Ashes series, nostalgic references to the days of Spofforth, Trumper, Bradman, Miller and other legends are what we hear about. Maybe, long term, for one-day international cricket we need to look towards establishing a constant worldwide competition in the manner of rugby union with its Six Nations and Tri Nations competitions.

The consistently huge crowds, keen interest, and moves such as that of the Australian one-day team to put their numbers on their caps suggest strongly that the fans and players respect the one-day game. Perhaps some officials and more media people need to do so as well.

The 1998–99 World Series, featuring Australia, England and Sri Lanka, was a typically vibrant tournament. For controversy, we had the story of Muttiah Muralitharan's bowling action, which came to a head in Adelaide when umpire Ross Emerson no-balled him and it seemed for a while that the Sri Lankans were going to abandon the match in protest. Away from that, the Englishmen started the tournament really well, winning four of their first five games. But eventually, the Poms were overwhelmed by us Australians.

I enjoyed being a part of the Australian side during this tournament, because after losing three of our first five games, we played some stunning cricket. With Steve Waugh out with a hamstring strain for most of the competition, Shane Warne led the team in his own style, while at the top of the order, Adam Gilchrist and Mark Waugh were sensational, and Glenn McGrath, with Warney in support, bowled beautifully. I contributed as well, hustling for 271 runs in the series for only twice out. Our competition victory was one of the sweetest of my career, and deserved to be recognised for the fine achievement it was.

Warney had missed the first half of the summer; he'd had shoulder surgery almost immediately after we returned from Sharjah in April and didn't make it back into the Test XI until the final Ashes Test in the first week of January. When he came back, initially it was as if he'd never been away. We bowled well but batted badly in the opening game, England getting home by seven runs. However, in our second game, at the SCG, Gilly smashed 131 from 118 balls, his fourth century in 12 months—he and Junior added 151 for the first wicket—and we won by eight wickets with nearly four overs to spare, despite the fact we were chasing 260.

Two days later, we thrashed England by nine wickets in Melbourne, the only downside coming when a section of the crowd went silly during our innings. I think they got bored because we were winning so easily, and decided to entertain themselves in an ugly manner, throwing golf balls and even snooker balls onto the field, dangerously close to the English outfielders. Why you'd take a snooker ball to the cricket is beyond me. It needed Warney to come out onto his home ground, don Mark Waugh's batting helmet (Junior was in the process of making a typically elegant 83 not out), and go down to the boundary rope to calm his fellow Victorians down.

One of the most interesting things about playing in front of a big crowd is how it reacts and treats you while you are out on the boundary. I have found that the reception you get depends to a large degree on which country you are playing in.

In a match in Peshawar during my first tour of Pakistan, for example, David Boon reacted in surprise and then anger after one of the crowd managed to catapult a firecracker to within five metres of him. I've seen crowds in the Caribbean explode when umpiring decisions haven't gone their way. Even playing in front of your home crowds can get testy if the team is doing badly or if you're having a poor game or spell yourself. Also awkward is the fact that you're not allowed to sign autographs while you're fielding, which can become an issue if you get spectators who have had a bit to drink or parents who have brought their kids to the game and can't believe that you'd ignore their future champions. Most players sign their fair share of autographs at the right time and place.

Overall, the toughest crowds I have come across have been in New Zealand. On one occasion at Eden Park, I was fielding on the boundary and heard all the regulation verbals, with the occasional lolly or apple thrown in my direction, usually narrowly missing me. Then, as I was walking in with the bowler, concentrating on what was taking place in the middle, I heard this enormous thud as something crashed to the ground near my feet. For a split second I thought the worst—was it a rock, full can of beer, hand grenade? Then I looked down to see this gorgeous four-kilo snapper glistening in the sunlight. Why the fish was wasted on me, I have no idea.

After that game in Melbourne, Tugga came back for the next two matches (we didn't win either, but that was hardly his fault), and then Warney led us to the title. I found him to be very clever and very effective as a captain. Tactically, he's spot on; he knows the game and has some terrific ideas. In many ways I found him similar to Mark Taylor, in the way he seemed to make the right decisions at the right times. If Shane is ever given the Australian captaincy, Test or one-day—not, I must stress very loudly, that I have any problem with Steve Waugh or Ricky Ponting—he would be an outstanding leader.

Before that World Series was over, we lost another match, against England in Sydney, and I found myself the subject of some criticism. And I had to cop it sweet, though I wondered whether the fact I'd succeeded in similar situations in the past was considered when the critics were making their post-match comments. Needing 283 to win, Mark Waugh and Darren Lehmann set up our pursuit brilliantly, but when Lehmann was dismissed for 76 in the 39th over, we needed 80 to win, with 68 deliveries still available. Slightly more than seven an over.

At the end we finished eight runs short of victory, and I was not out on 45, having faced 59 balls. We were only six down. It wasn't so much that I mismanaged the chase; I just batted poorly. I didn't hit even one boundary, which exposed my lack of timing, and though Greg Blewett hit 32 from 33 deliveries, we still needed 20 with two overs remaining, then 15 off the last one, from the left-arm spinner Ashley Giles. He held his nerve, and I had to wear the loss. For me, the defeat served as a reminder that you can't win all the time, rather than as an indication that my tactics were wrong. One of the reasons I believe that I do well at the end of the innings is that I am not afraid to let it get down to the wire, and that I'm patient under the pressure, believing that I can get my team home. In this match it didn't happen for me, but I can accept whatever criticism comes my way.

After losing narrowly to Sri Lanka in Hobart (another controversial fixture in which Arjuna Ranatunga was at his annoying best), we set off on a run of imposing form. Glenn McGrath took 5-40 against the Sri Lankans in Adelaide—firing the ball in at the batsmen's ribs with great effect—and in the last match before the finals Gilly became the first Australian to go past 150 in a one-day international, lashing 154 from 129 balls. That was some innings.

Glenn McGrath might not be as fast as, say, Shoaib Akhtar or Brett Lee, but he is still a phenomenal bowler. He just bowls good ball after good ball after good ball; his consistency is something to behold, he never complicates things too much, and he knows exactly what he's doing out there. But the consistency is the key for me, and one thing about him is that, while other bowlers might have a 'better' best ball that they can only produce on very rare occasions, Glenn can bowl his best delivery seemingly whenever he needs it. Thus, a great many of his deliveries can get you out. In any one over, you're very unlikely to get a loose one, while three or four balls are going to test you to the limit. Most bowlers can't do that more than once or twice an over, not over after over like Glenn can.

This high-class consistency is why his skills translate so well from Test cricket to one-day cricket. If he was consistently mediocre, batsmen would get used to him and eventually murder him. But because he is consistently bowling excellently, no one-day batsman can take to him, especially at the start of an innings when the ball is new. I've been asked whether 'Pigeon' would be of more value in the middle of an innings, to strangle the heart out of an innings, but I don't think so, not in most circumstances. He'd be good at these times, but the start and finish of a one-day innings are the crunch times. If your opponents begin at a rate of five, six or seven runs an over, especially if they do so without losing wickets, that start invariably acts as a springboard for a big innings total. It's difficult for a bowling side to arrest that sort of scoring-rate. Thus, it's important to use one of your best bowlers at the start. A slow start by the batsmen, especially if a couple of wickets go down as well, puts pressure on the middle order, and forces the remaining batsmen to play to your tune, not their own.

In the last 10 overs, you need your best bowlers to curtail a late assault; many are the times that I've seen the bowling team seemingly in control until the final 10 overs, when, left without their top-line performers to complete the innings, they allow the batting side to mount a fightback. In these situations, you need bowlers who can put the ball precisely and consistently in the right spot. A good example was our last-ball win at the SCG against the West Indies on New Year's Day 1996, which came about in part because Walsh and Ambrose had bowled most of their overs at the beginning. This isn't rocket science, but it does explain why Pigeon bowls most of his overs at the end and the beginning of a one-day innings.

Another question I've been often asked is who is the toughest bloke to face in the final overs of a one-day match. This can vary, depending on the situation, but I can narrow it down to two—Wasim Akram and Waqar Younis bowling in Pakistan with the ball swinging Irish. They're both very quick, can bowl lethal yorkers, and in their home conditions are not only able to get that reverse swing working big time, they can control it admirably. If the light is a little murky, as it can get late in the day, and the pitch is playing slow and low, as most pitches in Pakistan do, scoring big runs is nearly impossible.

Generally, the ball I find most difficult to score off at the end is the yorker. Very, very few bowlers can fire in yorker after yorker, getting the line and length exactly right, ball after ball in the final overs. A yorker, of course, is not too far removed from a half-volley or a full toss, and if you bowl too many of those at the death you'll inevitably go for plenty.

Back to the one-dayers in 1998–99, to the World Series finals. The first final, at the SCG, was a beauty, a tense occasion that could have gone either way until our two star bowlers—Warne and McGrath—stepped up and got us home. Earlier, I'd contributed 69 from 74 balls as we reached 8–232 from our 50 overs, which won me back the friends I'd lost when the Poms defeated us earlier in the series. It might have been my best one-day innings in Australia since the last-ball-four dig against the West Indies three years earlier, made on a pitch that was a little on the slow side and despite an outfield that was still damp after overnight and morning rain. I hit six fours and 32 singles, and enjoyed deflecting the English bowlers into the gaps in the legside field, no matter how much they concentrated on a line on or outside the off-stump. Throughout, I kept thinking that if I batted at a run a ball, then we'd finish with between 220 and 240, which we thought would be enough. And so it proved, but only just. One of the reasons I believe Australian teams play so well in crunch games is that we are taught to play to win at all levels of cricket. It begins with grade cricket, which is very competitive, followed by first-class cricket, which I believe has the right rules and structures to build a winning culture.

England batted very well, but we never panicked. At the conclusion of the 42nd over, they were 4–196, requiring only 4.62 runs an over to get home. Then Warney bowled a crucial over, taking two wickets while conceding only two runs, and the game changed. Next over, Brendon Julian took a brilliant catch, running 25 metres from deep long-off to dismiss Vince Wells, and we had Glenn McGrath in reserve to mop up the tail. In one spell of 21 deliveries, England lost five wickets for six runs.

Unfortunately, I had to watch this excitement from the dressing room, nursing a dislocated middle finger on my right hand. I'd made the mistake of trying to catch, while fielding at short midwicket, a fierce pull shot from Alec Stewart, and knew straightaway that I was in trouble. Dropped the catch, too, and the ball continued all the way to the boundary. The memories provoked by the photographs in the paper the next day, which showed the compound dislocation in all its gory detail, were almost as painful as the injury itself. So while the rest of the guys went to Melbourne, where we'd win decisively by 162 runs, I had to stay home. It was a very professional victory, which came about because we were able to raise our game at the crucial times, and was the twelfth time Australia had won the World Series (with its different names) in 20 seasons. It was a historic achievement, made in dramatic and entertaining style, one I think we had every right to celebrate.

AUSTRALIA V ENGLAND, CARLTON & UNITED SERIES FIRST FINAL, 1998–99
SYDNEY CRICKET GROUND
10 FEBRUARY 1999 (50-OVERS MATCH)
TOSS: AUSTRALIA

Australia innings

ME Waugh c Stewart b Wells	42
+AC Gilchrist b Gough	29
RT Ponting c Stewart b Wells	10
DS Lehmann c Mullally b Wells	19
DR Martyn c Stewart b Ealham	21
MG Bevan not out	69
S Lee c Fairbrother b Ealham	12
BP Julian c sub (BC Hollioake) b Ealham	12
*SK Warne b Gough	9
AC Dale not out	1
Extras (lb 6, w 1, nb 1)	8
Total (8 wickets, 50 overs)	232

DNB: GD McGrath
Fall: 1-40 (Gilchrist), 2-67 (Ponting), 3-98 (Waugh), 4-115 (Lehmann), 5-139 (Martyn), 6-176 (Lee), 7-199 (Julian), 8-222 (Warne)
Bowling: Gough 10-0-43-2, Mullally 7-0-42-0, Wells 10-2-30-3, Ealham 10-0-45-3, Croft 5-1-28-0, Hollioake 8-0-38-0

England innings

NV Knight b Dale	22
*+AJ Stewart c Waugh b Dale	27
GA Hick run out	42
N Hussain st Gilchrist b Warne	58
NH Fairbrother c Gilchrist b McGrath	8
VJ Wells c Julian b Lee	33
AJ Hollioake lbw Warne	0
MA Ealham c Gilchrist b McGrath	4
RDB Croft not out	12
D Gough b McGrath	0
AD Mullally b McGrath	7
Extras (lb 3, w 2, nb 4)	9
Total (all out, 49.2 overs)	222

Fall: 1-34 (Stewart), 2-67 (Knight), 3-114 (Hick), 4-131 (Fairbrother), 5-198 (Hussain), 6-198 (Hollioake), 7-198 (Wells), 8-204 (Ealham), 9-204 (Gough), 10-222 (Mullally)
Bowling: McGrath 9.2-1-45-4, Dale 10-0-33-2, Lee 7-1-29-1, Warne 10-0-40-2, Julian 4-0-28-0, Martyn 6-0-27-0, Lehmann 3-0-17-0

RESULT: AUSTRALIA WON BY 10 RUNS
UMPIRES: SJ DAVIS AND DB HAIR
MAN OF THE MATCH: MG BEVAN

GAME 20

I could have chosen to include in this book any one of three or four of the matches from this best-of-seven series, which featured some outstanding cricket, but also some of the ugliest crowd disturbances that have occurred in matches I've been a part of.

There was game five, at Georgetown, Guyana, which ended in chaotic circumstances as Steve Waugh and Shane Warne tried to complete an unlikely third run that would have tied the game. The crowd was in the process of invading the field, and in the confusion no one was sure what happened. More than likely, had the locals not come onto the field, Stephen would have been run out, but the match referee, Raman Subba Row from England, decided a tie was the fairest result. It wasn't the first time that there had been a pitch invasion in the late afternoon; perhaps Mr Subba Row was thinking that he might be teaching the locals a lesson if the result didn't go their way.

My view was that the crowd was just over anxious for the match to finish. They thought that their team had won, but their premature celebration marred the entire day. I can understand their exuberance, without condoning it, but at the same time, it would have been nice to see some safety and security for the players.

Then there was game seven, at Bridgetown in Barbados, when the mood changed to ugly after Sherwin Campbell was given out, run out, after a mid-pitch collision with Brendon Julian. For me, the events that followed this incident were far more shameful than those that took place in Guyana, because there were different reasons for this riot.

Earlier in the day, I'd been run out exactly the same way as Campbell had. I went to run, the bowler moved to his right, we collided, and I was stranded. When I was given out, I walked off. Campbell didn't. He stayed to put pressure on the umpire, and incite the crowd. We believed—correctly, I'm sure—that the umpire was in the best position to decide. The patrons, very clearly, thought their Sherwin was right and we were very wrong. Soon after, the guys fielding on the boundary had to dash from the outfield into the middle because the crowd were hand-grenading bottles and cans, and anything else they could get their hands on, onto the field. A quick mid-pitch team meeting, and we decided to seek the relative safety of the dressing room, but only after someone pointed out that we'd be OK because our rooms were in the members' area. Had we been obliged to venture near some other parts of the ground we might have stayed in the centre. Good plan? Hardly. As we approached the boundary, the members started throwing bottles at us as well, and Steve Waugh nearly wore one, thrown by a very well-known local cricket identity. Meanwhile, our wives in the grandstand were copping plenty as well.

The powers that be then decided, after a lengthy delay, that the game should continue, with Campbell reinstated, a course of action not all of us agreed with. Why? There was no guarantee that the crowd was going to behave, that more bottles weren't going to be thrown at the outfielders. Why reward such behaviour? I don't think sportsmen should be subjected to this sort of conduct. And no one could convince any of us that Campbell was entitled to be given such a break. But some local officials explained that all hell might break loose if we stayed in our rooms. So, in the interests of peace and goodwill, we did head back out there, to go through the motions as the West Indies went on to a very hollow victory.

In contrast, my most pleasurable memory of this series is the second game, in St George's, a match we won comfortably and in which I had the pleasure of sharing a long match-winning fifth-wicket partnership of 172 with one of my favourite cricketers, Darren Lehmann.

In a way, Boof is a similar sort of one-day batsman to me. He likes to improvise, doesn't necessarily have to smash the ball in the manner of an Adam Gilchrist, knows where the gaps are in the field. He scores quickly and is capable of being brutal with bowlers. He's also not scared to try new things, and he's got every shot. I like the way, late in his career, that he settled on a method of play in one-day cricket and stuck to it; that strength of character is what got him back into the Australian one-day XI and the Test squad. He's always been a very good one-day player and today is an outstanding one. In my view, he should have played many more one-day internationals.

When Boof made his superb hundred against the West Indies at St George's, from just 88 balls, he was fighting back after being sacked from the Test squad following the 1998–99 Ashes series in Australia. It was something of a rebound for the team as a whole, too, given that we'd lost the opening game of the one-day series in the Caribbean against England and the Test guys had been through a difficult four-match rubber that had ended two-all. Early on, things didn't look too promising here in St George's either, as we struggled to 4–116 in the 26th over, but then Darren took over, and we finished up with a then record total by Australia in a one-day international against the Windies.

Boof started by cutting his first ball for four, as if to announce this was going to be his day. I can picture him now, slashing the ball away for four and then taking a few strides down the pitch, shoulders back, jaws firmly clenched, in a way that suggested he did this sort of thing off every ball. More than a 100 runs later—his second century in one-day international cricket—he cut another ball to the backward-point boundary, to finish on 110, from 92 balls. It was fun to bat with him, especially in the final nine overs when we added 88 runs. There were a few boundaries in this period—five fours and a six to Boof, four fours to me—but also 29 singles; that is, on average, more than three ones an over. In those last nine overs, we scored at least a single off all but nine of the deliveries we faced.

The last over, bowled by Keith Arthurton, gave an indication of our styles as one-day batsmen. Arthurton bowls left-arm finger spin, spearing in the ball at this very late stage of a limited-overs innings. First ball, I gave myself some room and forced him through the covers and we dashed a two. Next ball, an easy single. Then Boof stepped back and pulled him down to long-on for another one. Fourth ball, I went down the pitch and drove him firmly, hoping for four, but it went straight to the deep midwicket fieldsman for one. Penultimate delivery, with a big gap on the deep third man boundary, Boof premeditated a reverse sweep, but missed, no run. And final ball, guessing that Arthurton would spear in at the leg stump, he gave himself room, but in fact the ball was aimed slightly outside off stump. He overbalanced, then lunged into a one-handed cut shot and did enough to get it away for four.

We were batting in a new stadium, located in one of the most picturesque venues in world cricket, just a lofted drive from the ocean. This was the first international match played in Grenada since 1983 (and only the second ever), and so important an event was it that the local Prime Minister, a cricket addict, declared the day a public holiday for the island's 94 000 residents. Sixteen thousand people turned up, testing the stadium's facilities to the max, and it all made for a party atmosphere and a famous day. By the time we arrived in the morning, the festivities were in full swing, the sounds of trumpets, cymbals, drums and whistles were reverberating around the place, and even as the local heroes' defeat became inevitable, the fun continued. A week and a half later, I couldn't help thinking how far removed the angry scenes in Georgetown and Bridgetown were from the happy days in St George's.

By and large, the West Indies is one of the better, more interesting tours. The people, whether they are or not, *seem* to be very relaxed and pretty cool. And the crowds are very animated, they really enjoy it. Though sometimes I wondered if cricket knowledge in the Caribbean had been clouded by those glory days in the 1970s and 1980s, when all their bowlers came out, day after day, and bowled fast and short and their batsmen whacked the bowlers all over the park. These days they haven't got the bowlers or the batsmen (Brian Lara apart) to do this, and as a consequence they sometimes seem lost. The fact that the rules now curtail the number of bouncers you can bowl hurts them because they haven't yet developed an alternative plan, and the fact that a specific number of overs needs to be bowled in a day hasn't helped either.

The thing about one-day cricket, if the game is played on a good batting wicket, the odds are loaded in the batsmen's favour. With restrictions on the number of short balls you can bowl, the wide rule—especially down the legside—policed so rigorously, and the batsmen forced by the nature of the game to attack, bowlers have their work cut out. What this means is that the great bowlers—stars such as McGrath, Warne, Pollock, Ambrose, Walsh, Wasim Akram—really stand out, while many bowlers who can do well in Test cricket struggle in the one-dayers. This is especially true of really quick guys who can't adjust to situations where their line and length have to be disciplined. Bowlers in one-day cricket who give top-class batsmen gilt-edged opportunities to attack get slaughtered, whatever pace they bowl at. I reckon some of the inexperienced West Indies quicks who've been picked in recent years to replace the legends of the previous era have learnt this lesson the hard way.

This match in St George's was a match that demonstrated how easy it is for things to change in a one-day match. The key here was that there was much more depth in the Australian bowling attack—guys such as Shane Lee and the Waugh twins supported Shane Warne very well in the middle overs—whereas we were able to pick up some cheap runs against bowlers who probably weren't up to international class. After 25 overs of the West Indies' innings, they were 3–118, three runs more than Australia was at the corresponding stage, with the same number of wickets in hand. Both teams then lost another wicket, but from there things went very differently: Boof and I batted for the rest of the innings for 4–288, whereas the Windies lost Carl Hooper and Arthurton straightaway to fall to 6–140 and never recovered. Not even an amusing cameo from Curtly Ambrose, which included one moment when he tried to smash Brendon Julian into the sea, only for his bat to shatter into pieces, could save him. Courtney Walsh brought out four possible replacement bats for him and Ambrose showed how good he was at selecting timber by whacking the next ball way over long-on for six. The big crowd was in uproar.

I guess this sort of thing could have happened in a four- or five-day match. Some cricket buffs probably couldn't care, but those seeking value for their entertainment dollar certainly do.

AUSTRALIA V WEST INDIES, SECOND ONE-DAY INTERNATIONAL, 1998–99 QUEEN'S PARK, ST GEORGE'S, GRENADA 14 APRIL 1999 (50-OVERS MATCH) TOSS: AUSTRALIA

Australia innings
+AC Gilchrist c Chanderpaul b Hooper	17
ME Waugh c & b Hooper	41
DR Martyn b King	28
DS Lehmann not out	110
*SR Waugh c Lara b King	0
MG Bevan not out	72
Extras (lb 6, w 8, nb 6)	20
Total (4 wickets, 50 overs)	288

DNB: S Lee, BP Julian, PR Reiffel, SK Warne, DW Fleming
Fall: 1-30 (Gilchrist), 2-85 (ME Waugh), 3-108 (Martyn), 4-116 (SR Waugh)
Bowling: Ambrose 10-0-47-0, King 10-0-53-2, Hooper 10-0-66-2, Arthurton 8-0-43-0, Bryan 7-0-41-0, Simmons 5-0-32-0

West Indies innings
SL Campbell b Lee	46
S Chanderpaul c Lee b Fleming	0
*BC Lara b Fleming	9
+JC Adams b Warne	40
CL Hooper c & b SR Waugh	17
SC Williams c sub (TM Moody) b Warne	25
KLT Arthurton b Lee	0
PV Simmons c Lee b Reiffel	39
HR Bryan lbw Warne	6
CEL Ambrose run out	23
RD King not out	12
Extras (lb 3, w 14, nb 8)	25
Total (all out, 47.3 overs)	242

Fall: 1-3 (Chanderpaul), 2-18 (Lara), 3-102 (Adams), 4-125 (Campbell), 5-135 (Hooper), 6-140 (Arthurton), 7-174 (Williams), 8-183 (Bryan), 9-215 (Simmons), 10-242 (Ambrose)
Bowling: Fleming 8-1-45-2, Reiffel 8-0-53-1, Julian 7-0-49-0, Martyn 2-0-5-0, Warne 10-2-39-3, ME Waugh 3-0-13-0, Lee 6-0-22-2, SR Waugh 3.3-0-13-1

RESULT: AUSTRALIA WON BY 46 RUNS
UMPIRES: SA BUCKNOR AND W DOCTROVE
MAN OF THE MATCH: DS LEHMANN

GAME 21

AUSTRALIA V SOUTH AFRICA
WORLD CUP SUPER SIX MATCH
HEADINGLEY
13 JUNE 1999

For me, the 1999 World Cup was a huge occasion. For the team, too, though maybe for different reasons. Personally, I was going to be playing on the biggest stage possible, at a time when some critics—including my captain—were describing me as the finest one-day batsman in the world. The tournament was a showcase for the style of cricket with which I was making my name. And I knew from my experiences in 1996 that this was also an event to be enjoyed.

Within 12 months of our eventual victory in this tournament, the Australian team was almost universally regarded as the best one-day team on the planet. The World Cup triumph was the beginning of this. Consequently, most people who look back on this time forget the fact that we went into the World Cup with something of a cloud over our head. The debate about having two separate teams had still not abated completely, while Steve Waugh had not had a controversy-free time of it as captain in the West Indies. A lot of people wanted to compare his leadership to his predecessor, Mark Taylor, and not too favourably, but I thought this was unfair as they are skippers with very different styles.

In the Test series, which many observers had expected Australia to win easily, the guys had been forced to come back from 1–2 down to level the four-Test rubber. In the one-dayers, we'd finished at three games apiece, with that controversial 'tie' in Guyana the result that kept us level. Shane Warne had been left out of the team for the final Test. Stephen's forthright comments about the riot in Bridgetown—comments we supported to a man—had not gone down too well with the local authorities. When we started the World Cup slowly, losing to New Zealand and Pakistan, the critics had a field day.

I'd been looking forward to the 1999 Cup since just about the day after we lost the final to Sri Lanka in Lahore three-and-a-bit years before. Maybe that's what cost us in the early matches; we put too much pressure on ourselves in the lead up, to the point that when we played the early games we weren't playing for the moment. Instead, we had our eyes on bigger games further into the event. After losing to Pakistan, we faced elimination if we lost another game, but a big win against Bangladesh and then a comfortable, if somewhat controversial, defeat of the West Indies at Old Trafford got us through to the 'Super Six'.

It was intriguing for me, watching the way the guys approached this tournament. Warney was still coming back from his shoulder operation, and though he had bowled well in the one-dayers in the West Indies, I felt his confidence was still a little shaken after his omission from the Test team. Stephen seemed determined, maybe too determined, to make his mark as a captain. Some guys appeared preoccupied with their own roles, rather than the overall team performance. These distractions hindered our early efforts, and nowhere was this more apparent than in our fielding, which by our standards was terrible. We were fretting over rather than enjoying our cricket. We needed to relax.

I remember having a chat to Stephen after our first game, where we weren't very impressive in defeating Scotland. In his diary of the tour, he wrote that during our conversation I said to him, 'Fielding is a real guide to a team's togetherness, because it is the only facet of the game that you truly do for the team and don't get statistically rewarded for, as a consequence of good play'. This is something I have always believed in strongly; the fact we were talking along these lines reflects the concern we all had for our display, and also for the overriding mood within the squad. At this stage we didn't have the mix within the XI right (that was corrected when Tom Moody came into the team for our fourth match, as the fifth bowler, batting 7), and we weren't gelling as a unit.

As I said, we went into the game against the West Indies needing a victory to stay in the tournament, and when we dismissed them for just 110 (Glenn McGrath 5–14, Shane Warne 3–11) we'd gone a long way to achieving our objective. Curtly came out firing and we found ourselves 4–62, but Stephen and I steadied the ship and at 4–90 we were just about over the line.

At this point we adopted what proved to be a very unpopular strategy. The way the tournament worked, the top three teams from the two qualifying groups went through to the second round, the so-called Super Six. If teams were level on their group table after the first-round matches, 'net run-rate' (runs per over scored divided by runs per over conceded) would be used to determine who went through. Into the Super Six, qualifiers would play the teams that had made it from the other group. Each team also carried forward to the Super Six points and run-rate from their group matches against the other teams that had qualified from their group. Still with me?

It was to our advantage that the West Indies, who we were certain to defeat, went through rather than New Zealand, who had beaten us earlier on. The West Indies were on six points, New Zealand on four, but with a group game still to play against Scotland, a match they were very likely to win. We therefore wanted the Windies to have as high a run-rate as possible, so long as it was less than ours (our victory over them took us to six points, too), to make it as hard as possible for the Kiwis to make it through. Still, still with me? Competitions with rules and conditions this complicated inevitably result in controversy, as was demonstrated again in Australia in 2001–02 when they introduced bonus points into the VB Series. So Stephen and I put on the brakes and stonewalled to victory, going from 4–90 to 4–111 in almost 20 overs.

We were just playing to our best advantage, within the rules that had been presented to us. The fault, surely, would have been not trying to maximise our chances of winning the tournament. In fact, we finished the game faster than we should have; we could have really drawn the process out and made it even harder for the New Zealanders (not that it mattered in the end, they thrashed Scotland to make it through), but I think the hecklers got to us a little and we won the match in the 41st over, still only four wickets down.

We went into the Super Six knowing we needed to prevail in every game if we wanted to win the whole thing. In the end, I believe this worked to our advantage, because we became used to the win-or-you're-out scenario while our biggest threats—Pakistan and South Africa—were cruising towards the semi-finals. One slip and we were gone. But we beat India and Zimbabwe fairly comfortably, to give us four wins on the trot, and set up what was for us a sudden-death Super Six game against South Africa at Headingley.

What a match this turned out to be, made famous for Steve Waugh's great innings, which took us to one of the finest victories I have ever been involved in, achieved against an outstanding side who were very confident and in impressive form.

The biggest thing we had in our favour going into the game was a feeling that had permeated through the entire squad, a belief that whenever we played South Africa in a big match we would come through. We felt that then, we feel it even more firmly today. But this was a little bit different because South Africa didn't have to win (they were assured of a semi-final place), whereas we most certainly did. I thought that could prove to be significant, because they had no pressure on them, they could just play.

And for a long while, that's how it turned out. As I knew from my time in Yorkshire, anything over 250 is more than likely a winning score in a one-day game at Headingley. When Lance Klusener blasted away at the end of their innings for 36 from 21 balls, our target was

272—as I said, usually a winning score. But not this time: the difference this time was that Stephen stepped up to play the one-day innings of his life. This knock represented a real turnaround for him as a one-day batsman; from this day on he became a great player, rather than just a very good one. His display was almost unbelievable; he played in a way which I had never seen him play before, as if he had decided as he walked out to bat that his entire career as a one-day cricketer and captain was on the line, that he had to be bold, back himself, go down fighting. He won the game for us, keeping us alive in the World Cup and providing us all with the best demonstration of the value of self-belief we could ever wish to see.

I came out to bat when Ricky Ponting was dismissed, when we needed 98 runs with 95 balls still available. Punter had played a crucial hand, rebuilding the innings after we lost three early wickets. The way he and Tugga had batted slowly at first (scoring 22 runs from one spell of 10 overs) before mounting a savage counterattack against the bowling they had identified as the South Africans' weakest link was what I would describe as classic one-day batting. I knew I had to get on with it straightaway, no time to settle in, had to play shots that I wouldn't normally play. I think I went over the top early on, which I rarely do.

I was helped by the fact that Stephen was in total control. His famous confrontation with Herschelle Gibbs had already occurred, when he reputedly told Gibbs that he had 'dropped the World Cup' when he dropped him; I'm not sure exactly what he said, but the mistake did turn the game.

I got myself out for 27 in the 46th over, and was furious afterwards. At this time, the required run-rate was bang on six an over, I was feeling good and Steve was invincible. First ball of the over, I hit Hansie Cronje for four, lofted to within a few metres of the long-off boundary, to release the pressure a fraction, but became a little indecisive and played a ridiculous shot two balls later, to be caught by Darryl Cullinan at midwicket. Part of my brain was thinking that I needed to attack Cronje there and then, another part was trying to calm me down, saying that the four I'd hit had got us back on the run-a-ball track, that we could get it in singles.

It was a shot that I don't think I had ever attempted in a one-day international before. I walked off the field really pissed off, thinking over and over, 'Why did I do that? Of all times to do it . . . Why now?', and remained in the change room until just before the winning runs were scored, all the while believing that I had cost us the game. I should have been there at the end. Instead, Tom Moody entered to help Steve get the final 25 runs we needed, which they did with a calm and assurance that reflected the fact that they are two very sensible cricketers. Later, I learnt that even a brilliant Shaun Pollock over, three from the end, couldn't stop our victory march. Seven runs came from the second last over, then eight from the first four balls of the 50th over and we won with two balls to spare. In the semi-finals we'd be facing . . . South Africa!

In my view, Steve Waugh became a great one-day cricketer at this World Cup. Before that, he was just a very good one. During the three-and-a-bit years since the previous Cup, as the cricket world gradually came to accept that one-day cricket was a different game with different skills, Tugga really went out of his way to learn the art of one-day cricket and how he could improve his one-day batting. Until the Australian team 'split' into two separate entities, as a senior batsman in the Test team who could also bowl 10 overs and field well, Stephen was just about automatically guaranteed a berth in the one-day starting line-up, so he didn't have to think so much about what it takes to succeed in one-day cricket. None of the established Test guys did. But as soon as he started thinking seriously about one-day batting—and because he's a clear thinker on the game and an immensely talented cricketer—he quickly became one of the sport's best one-day players.

In recent times, he's received many plaudits for being 'mentally tough'. Commentators writing and talking about this game kept referring to Stephen's mental toughness when trying to analyse what separates him from the rest of us. And Stephen *is* mentally tough—to get to the top of the ladder, as Stephen has done in cricket, you need to be able to think clearly and remain perceptive and focused in pressure situations. These are not easy skills to learn. Tugga's career is proof of how much he has grown, as a player and a person, how strong he has become. For some people, being mentally tough comes naturally; these are the players who succeed from day one and keep succeeding. Sachin Tendulkar is an excellent example of this, so is Shane Warne. Others, including Steve Waugh, have to work very, very hard, go through some tough times, and make some major changes to their approach, their makeup, even their personality, before they achieve their success. This can require an incredible amount of willpower and honesty, traits Stephen has in abundance.

His great career—and his great innings, especially the one he made at Headingley that kept us in the 1999 World Cup—underlines the fact that if you want to be the best you need to ask yourself questions all the time, about your preparation, your focus, your ambitions, and always be honest with the answers.

AUSTRALIA V SOUTH AFRICA, WORLD CUP SUPER SIX MATCH, 1999
HEADINGLEY, LEEDS
13 JUNE 1999 (50-OVERS MATCH)
TOSS: SOUTH AFRICA

South Africa innings

G Kirsten c Ponting b Reiffel	21
HH Gibbs b McGrath	101
DJ Cullinan b Warne	50
*WJ Cronje lbw Warne	0
JN Rhodes c ME Waugh b Fleming	39
L Klusener c Warne b Fleming	36
SM Pollock b Fleming	3
+MV Boucher not out	0
Extras (lb 7, w 8, nb 6)	21
Total (7 wickets, 50 overs)	271

DNB: N Boje, S Elworthy, AA Donald
Fall: 1-45 (Kirsten), 2-140 (Cullinan), 3-141 (Cronje), 4-219 (Gibbs), 5-250 (Rhodes), 6-271 (Klusener), 7-271 (Pollock)
Bowling: McGrath 10-0-49-1, Fleming 10-0-57-3, Reiffel 9-0-47-1, Moody 8-1-56-0, Warne 10-1-33-2, Bevan 3-0-22-0

Australia innings

ME Waugh run out	5
+AC Gilchrist b Elworthy	5
RT Ponting c Donald b Klusener	69
DR Martyn c Boje b Elworthy	11
*SR Waugh not out	120
MG Bevan c Cullinan b Cronje	27
TM Moody not out	15
Extras (lb 6, w 7, nb 7)	20
Total (5 wickets, 49.4 overs)	272

DNB: SK Warne, PR Reiffel, DW Fleming, GD McGrath
Fall: 1-6 (Gilchrist), 2-20 (ME Waugh), 3-48 (Martyn), 4-174 (Ponting), 5-247 (Bevan)
Bowling: Pollock 9.4-0-45-0, Elworthy 10-1-46-2, Donald 10-0-43-0, Klusener 10-0-53-1, Cronje 7-0-50-1, Boje 3-0-29-0

RESULT: AUSTRALIA WON BY FIVE WICKETS
UMPIRES: S VENKATARAGHAVAN (IND) AND P WILLEY
MAN OF THE MATCH: SR WAUGH

GAME 22

AUSTRALIA V SOUTH AFRICA
WORLD CUP SEMI-FINAL
EDGBASTON
17 JUNE 1999

I went into this semi-final much more confident than I had been before the Super Six game against South Africa. We had the momentum, had showed that we were invigorated by the pressure, while South Africa now had to contend with the unique stress of a knockout situation. Since they had re-entered international cricket in 1992, they had never beaten us in a head-to-head series, in Tests or one-dayers. Yet many times during what evolved into a classic match, it looked as if our magic run was coming to an end.

For me, it was not unlike the semi-final against the West Indies in 1996. We batted first, and crashed to 4–68 before Steve Waugh and I revived the innings. Before the game we had talked about the Edgbaston track as being worth around 250, now we had to modify our expectations. I thought anything over 200 would be a bonus, and batted accordingly.

In such situations, the thought eats away at you: is that new target really enough? I was concerned that I was going too slowly, but at the same time focused on the fact that I needed to keep my wicket intact.

I work on the theory that sometimes you have to do less than what your conscience is nagging you to do. I knew we had to post a score, and have learnt from experience that setting a realistic target in this way is what works best for me. I don't think a lot of players work it out like that; instead, they just accept whatever comes. Each to their own.

I must admit that I was a little bemused when I first went out there, because South Africa decided to try the old bang-'em-in-short trick. They were about two years too late. Jacques Kallis put in a short leg and started firing them in at my ribs, at a time when the deck was still doing a bit. To be honest I wasn't just bemused, I was a tad indignant that they'd resort to this. It fired me up, and I hit Kallis for a couple of fours, key boundaries that helped change the mood.

I've rarely felt as good in a big game as I did that day. Stephen and I communicated really well when we were batting together; we were on the same page, working together to get us a total we thought we could defend. In terms of runs per ball, this probably doesn't compare with some of my more dynamic innings, but I felt I got this one pretty right, and the 65 ranks as one of my most satisfying knocks. After Steve and Tom Moody were both dismissed with the score at 158, Warney and I added 49 for the seventh wicket, and I scored the majority of them, until I was caught behind as we hustled for every run beyond 200 that we could muster.

The South Africans had got the ball to seam about a bit, so we thought our main attacking forces would be Glenn McGrath and Damien Fleming with the new ball. But when they bowled, it was as if the wicket had flattened out in the break between innings, and Herschelle Gibbs and Gary Kirsten were into them. In nine overs, they belted 45 runs, and almost in desperation our captain turned to Shane Warne. This, most certainly, had not been in the pre-match game plan.

Warney had been a little out of form, seemingly disillusioned about his future, perhaps not sure about his shoulder. But now he stepped up and gave the ball a real rip, and the results were fantastic. Gibbs had looked in complete control, but straightaway Warney knocked him over with a leg break that looked to me to be every bit as lethal as the famous ball that bowled Mike Gatting at Old Trafford in 1993. Instantly, the mood changed, which to me reflects a simple fact of cricket—that even one wicket can alter the balance of the contest. You should never give up. The guys out in the middle might be going along fine, feeling no pressure, but in comes a new batsman, someone who's been sitting in the change room, thinking about the situation, about what he needs to do, about what might happen if he fails, about how good the bowling is looking. Inevitably, a wicket boosts the bowling team, so that this new batsman comes out to find the fieldsmen chirpy, the bowler aggressive. One more wicket, your wicket, and the game could be lost. Warney took two more wickets, Kirsten and Hansie Cronje, all within his first three overs. When Cullinan was run out for 6 (by a direct throw from mid-off by yours truly), his nerve seeming to fail him, South Africa were 4–61.

I didn't think we were far in front at this stage—the game was really back on something of an even keel. After all, earlier in the day, Stephen and I had been in a similar position to the one in which Jonty Rhodes and Jacques Kallis now found themselves. Together, these two very good players added 84, before Paul Reiffel dismissed Rhodes in the 41st over. By the start of over 45, Shaun Pollock and Kallis had taken the score to 5–162. Warney had one over remaining, Pollock was on strike.

The first ball went for two, the second for six, the third for four. It was starting to slip away, but then the great leg-spinner regrouped. A single, a dot ball, and then, his last ball of the innings—Kallis was deceived into spooning a catch to Steve Waugh at midwicket.

In strode Lance Klusener like a colossus, having already done enough in this World Cup to be named the player of the tournament. He'd earned that accolade by smashing the ball out of the middle of the bat every single time he swung it, and from the jump nothing changed here. Flemo was belted away to deep midwicket, then later in the same over Pollock was bowled off the inside edge. On the boundary, I remember thinking, 'We're going to win this. No, we're going to lose this. No, we're going to win this.' Every over.

With hindsight, we might have made a mistake by not putting more pressure on Klusener. While Mark Boucher, their very good keeper-batsman, struggled to get the ball off the square, Klusener kept swinging away, everything powering off the sweet spot of that big bat of his. (It wasn't until we brought the field in, right at the death when we had no alternative, that Klusener suddenly looked mortal again.) Boucher's stumps were shattered by the second ball of the 49th over, bowled by Glenn McGrath, 8–196; then Steve Elworthy was run out at the bowler's end from the fourth, but off the fifth Klusener clubbed a full-pitched delivery out in the direction of Paul Reiffel at long-on. In all my life I have never seen a shot like that one; it just kept going and going, like the proverbial tracer bullet, and Pistol misjudged it, coming in until, as the ball flew at him straight between the eyes, he realised he was in too close. Throwing his hands up, all he could do was deflect it over the boundary rope. For six! The game changed again. A single off the last ball, and South Africa needed nine to win.

Because we'd finished higher on the Super Six table than South Africa, a tie was all we needed to reach the final, a fact we were well aware of. Damien Fleming was the bowler, another repeat from Chandigarh in 1996. Only this time, for the first three deliveries, it seemed the story would be far different. Flem went round the wicket and Klusener hit two near yorkers for four to tie the scores at 211. What to do? We had to bring the field up, and this is where the equation changed. Instead of continuing to bang away, it seemed Klusener changed his approach, maybe looking for a one through the field to get his team into the final. It was as if he'd suddenly realised that he was going to win the game, whereas previously he'd been just swinging away, seeing what might happen if he chanced his arm. When you don't think you're a chance to win, you often don't put any pressure on yourself, and you can end up getting pretty close. But that's different to actually achieving the victory. A lot different.

Another key was communication, or, in the case of the last South African pair—Klusener and Allan Donald—lack of communication. I have no idea what they discussed between deliveries during that dramatic final over, but it couldn't have had much to do with what they intended to do to win the game. If I am ever in the same situation, I can guarantee you that I will at least be on the same wavelength as my batting partner.

Third delivery of the over, Klusener half swung at the ball, and it dribbled towards mid-on, not far from the stumps at the bowler's end. Darren Lehmann dashed in and in one motion grabbed at the ball and threw it at the stumps. He actually had more time than he thought, because Donald had started on an impossible run. Boof's shy missed, Donald snuck back, smiling sheepishly, as if he'd dodged a bullet. I figured our last winning chance had gone.

The tension was extraordinary. Flem pitched right up, and Klusener miscued again, straight up the pitch. And ran! Donald, recalling his near miss the ball before, dived back for the safety of the bowler's end; Mark Waugh, in from mid-off, gathered the ball and flicked it back to Flem at the stumps at the bowler's end; Klusener kept running, Donald dropped his bat and began running disconsolately to the other end; we all yelled in unison, 'Keeper's end! Keeper's end!' And Flem, calm as you like, rolled the ball down to Adam Gilchrist, who broke the stumps with Donald in mid-pitch. I just ran to the bloke nearest to me, can't remember who it was, and screamed in delight. This euphoria was one of the best feelings I have ever had in my life. And then we ran for the change rooms, dodging the spectators who had raced onto the ground, sat on a bench, drew breath and wondered, 'How the hell did we get away with that?'

It would have been wonderful to have been able to sit back and celebrate that 'victory', but with the final coming three days later, everyone was quickly focused on what we still had to do. The Pakistanis had been playing awesome cricket, their team included some superb players, and we were wary of the fact that it seemed as if everything they were trying was coming off. They were really confident, whereas I thought the game was evenly poised. However, my opinion changed before the first over of the match was completed, because Glenn McGrath's early deliveries revealed that the Lord's wicket had some genuine carry in it and plenty of bounce. It hadn't looked as if it would play that way beforehand. This is the sort of pitch we're used to, one the Pakistanis struggle on. It's the same when the teams from the sub-continent come to Australia and struggle to adapt. I knew we'd win that match from that moment on, maybe not as easily as we eventually did, but I knew we'd win.

Pakistan were bowled out for just 132, and although Wasim Akram and Shoaib Akhtar came out and bowled very quickly, Gilly rediscovered his best form, smashing a quickfire 54, and we won by eight wickets, Boof hitting the winning runs. The ease of our win meant the final was in some ways something of an anti-climax, but we didn't care, because the final was just a small part of the journey that was our World Cup. I've been asked if I felt any disappointment, because I never had the chance to bat or bowl or take a catch in the final. My reply is simple: I've played in winning teams and losing teams, and I much prefer to play in a winning team.

We all do.

AUSTRALIA V SOUTH AFRICA, WORLD CUP SEMI-FINAL, 1999
EDGBASTON, BIRMINGHAM
17 JUNE 1999 (50-OVERS MATCH)
TOSS: SOUTH AFRICA

Australia innings

+AC Gilchrist c Donald b Kallis	20
ME Waugh c Boucher b Pollock	0
RT Ponting c Kirsten b Donald	37
DS Lehmann c Boucher b Donald	1
*SR Waugh c Boucher b Pollock	56
MG Bevan c Boucher b Pollock	65
TM Moody lbw Pollock	0
SK Warne c Cronje b Pollock	18
PR Reiffel b Donald	0
DW Fleming b Donald	0
GD McGrath not out	0
Extras (b 1, lb 6, w 3, nb 6)	16
Total (all out, 49.2 overs)	213

Fall: 1-3 (ME Waugh), 2-54 (Ponting), 3-58 (Lehmann), 4-68 (Gilchrist), 5-158 (SR Waugh), 6-158 (Moody), 7-207 (Warne), 8-207 (Reiffel), 9-207 (Fleming), 10-213 (Bevan)
Bowling: Pollock 9.2-1-36-5, Elworthy 10-0-59-0, Kallis 10-2-27-1, Donald 10-1-32-4, Klusener 9-1-50-0, Cronje 1-0-2-0

South Africa innings

G Kirsten b Warne	18
HH Gibbs b Warne	30
DJ Cullinan run out	6
*WJ Cronje c ME Waugh b Warne	0
JH Kallis c SR Waugh b Warne	53
JN Rhodes c Bevan b Reiffel	43
SM Pollock b Fleming	20
L Klusener not out	31
+MV Boucher b McGrath	5
S Elworthy run out	1
AA Donald run out	0
Extras (lb 1, w 5)	6
Total (all out, 49.4 overs)	213

Fall: 1-48 (Gibbs), 2-53 (Kirsten), 3-53 (Cronje), 4-61 (Cullinan), 5-145 (Rhodes), 6-175 (Kallis), 7-183 (Pollock), 8-196 (Boucher), 9-198 (Elworthy), 10-213 (Donald)
Bowling: McGrath 10-0-51-1, Fleming 8.4-1-40-1, Reiffel 8-0-28-1, Warne 10-4-29-4, ME Waugh 8-0-37-0, Moody 5-0-27-0

RESULT: MATCH TIED (AUSTRALIA PROGRESS TO FINAL)
UMPIRES: DR SHEPHERD AND S VENKATARAGHAVAN (IND)
MAN OF THE MATCH: SK WARNE

GAME 23

AUSTRALIA V ZIMBABWE
THIRD ONE-DAY INTERNATIONAL
HARARE
24 OCTOBER 1999

This might seem like a strange game to include in a 'most memorable' matches book—we won a fairly mundane game very comfortably, by nine wickets, to complete a 3–0 clean sweep in this short series, so there was little drama. I did score 77 not out, so it was a good game for me, and Ricky Ponting was brilliant in making his 87 from 110 balls. And Glenn McGrath was at his persistent best, conceding just 18 runs from his 10 overs. But there are a number of reasons why I decided to include this game.

For starters, I always love batting with Ricky Ponting. Punter is somewhere between Adam Gilchrist and me as a one-day batsman, able to hit hard and often if the situation requires that kind of bold approach, but able to work the ones and twos as well. He also has good instincts and a sharp cricket brain, something that comes out when he's plotting an innings out in the middle, and gives every indication that he'll be an excellent captain.

As we all know, Gilly scores his runs at an incredible rate, but a trade-off for that is that he can be a little inconsistent. I must stress that I'm not being critical here—if I was a selector and Gilly was available to me, he would be opening the batting in every game without fail because of his ability to turn a match. But with this increased scoring-rate comes an increased risk. I go the other way: my scoring-rate is very calculated, determined by the match situation, which means that I'm more consistent than Gilly but, at the same time, I'm much less likely to hurt our opponents by belting runs at a rapid rate. Punter is a batsman with the flexibility and range of strokes to be able to adapt his game to whatever situation confronts him, and the cricket smarts to know what to do every time.

It's important that a one-day batting line-up contains an adaptability to handle all situations, and Punter is one of the most adaptable batsmen I have ever played with. I don't think a team full of Michael Bevans could win all the time, but neither could a team full of Adam Gilchrists. A team full of Ricky Pontings might have more chance of success, because he has such a broad skills base. That said, in the Australian team, we never expect guys to play in a manner different to the way that got them into the team in the first place, but we do have a broad enough variety of skills that we can adapt to any equation.

If you have been chosen for the team because of the way you have been playing, it would be cruel to suddenly be asked to play in a way foreign to your instincts, in a manner that doesn't exploit your strengths. What the current Australian team does is try to refine players' styles, and broaden their skills base, but it never tries to turn black into white. Current coach John Buchanan uses every new piece of technology he can get his hands on, covers every angle, and uses what I like to call a 'business' approach in sport. He's calm, clever, thoughtful and thorough. And ambitious, in that he wants the team to be absolutely as good as it can be. But he never forgets that you have to work with what you've got.

One of our opponents in this game, Zimbabwe's best ever player Andy Flower, played a lone hand of 99 not out after Steve Waugh won the toss and sent our hosts in. Now, in one sense it is very difficult for me to pass judgement on Andy Flower, because Australia has played so little cricket against Zimbabwe. There was the World Series in 1994–95, when the Australian Cricket Board felt it needed to include an Australia A team to bolster interest in the competition, and then the 2000–01 series when they again failed to make the finals. There have been occasional matches in the World Cup, including a game in the 1999 Cup when we defeated them in a Super Six match at Lord's, and a handful of other one-day matches in tournaments across the cricket globe. Only once have the two countries squared off in a Test match, when Australia won comfortably in Harare on this brief 1999 tour. So I haven't seen too much of Andy Flower, but what I have seen has impressed me.

He has put up some amazing numbers in Test cricket over the past couple of years. His Test batting average is well above 50 (at 30 June 2002 it was 52.30, his having scored 4655 runs in 61 Tests since his debut in Zimbabwe's first ever Test match appearance, in 1992), which is especially good for a bloke who has also often kept wicket. Indeed, he is one of only four men to score more than 2000 runs, average more than 50 with the bat and complete a stumping in Test cricket (Adam Gilchrist, Javed Miandad, who only stumped one unfortunate batsman, and Sir Clyde Walcott are the others). When he was named international cricketer of the year for 2001, I think a number of people stopped and asked, hang on, what has he done? And what he had done was score, in one run of 11 Tests in 2000 and 2001, 1466 runs at a very tidy average of 112.77, including seven fifties, four centuries and one double century. Never once in this golden run was he dismissed for less than 23. Only twice in a completed innings did he fail to reach 45. And remember, in all this time he never got to face Zimbabwe's bowling attack, which might be on the improve but is still not the most lethal in the game.

He might be more effective in Test cricket than one-day cricket, but he is still one helluva player. One thing that interests me about him is that he probably has the best reverse sweep in cricket. To have reached that status with a shot that is still not considered conventional—and has been condemned by many critics at different times—suggests to me that: one, he must have a lot of confidence; and two, he must practise it a lot. Confidence, of course, is often a product of good form, and, as his figures suggest, he's been in good form for a while. The fact that he practises a shot outside the norm reflects an approach to the one-day game that will become more popular in the seasons ahead. As teams search for an advantage, they'll rehearse unusual moves, teach themselves rare skills that will give them an edge, not just tinker briefly with radical ideas, but work on them and constantly modify them until they've got them right.

The 'principles' will always stay the same. There is never a need to complicate things unnecessarily. But there can be times in a one-day match where you need to try something different, to throw something else into the equation, such as a reverse sweep. If you're facing a spinner and there's only one guy behind gully, then there are opportunities to get four runs down to deep third man. But the time has to be right; at other times, it may be more prudent to keep getting those singles, and wait for the loose one outside off stump that you can hit backward of point anyway, without any risk. Still, in such circumstances, it may in the future be possible that a batsman akin to baseball's 'switch hitter'— able to bat both left and right handed—might be an answer, to break up a field, or change the tempo. Similarly, in the field, will come the day when players can throw left and right handed. John Buchanan is a firm believer in encouraging the development of this skill. A generation or two from now we might be breeding plenty of guys with such talent, and pondering how one-dimensional were the fieldsmen of the early 21st century.

Which is awesome when you think how much the overall fielding standard has improved already, compared to where it was 20 or 30 years ago.

AUSTRALIA V ZIMBABWE, THIRD ONE-DAY INTERNATIONAL, 1999–2000
HARARE SPORTS CLUB
24 OCTOBER 1999 (50-OVERS MATCH)
TOSS: AUSTRALIA

Zimbabwe innings

*ADR Campbell b McGrath	18
NC Johnson c Warne b McGrath	5
TN Madondo c Gilchrist b Moody	6
+A Flower not out	99
GW Flower c Martyn b Symonds	21
MW Goodwin c Symonds b Warne	14
AM Blignaut c Bevan b Warne	1
JA Rennie run out	10
GB Brent lbw Moody	0
AR Whittall run out	1
DT Mutendera not out	8
Extras (lb 7, w 6, nb 4)	17
Total (9 wickets, 50 overs)	200

Fall: 1-24 (Johnson), 2-28 (Campbell), 3-38 (Madondo), 4-81 (GW Flower), 5-120 (Goodwin), 6-125 (Blignaut), 7-154 (Rennie), 8-156 (Brent), 9-167 (Whittall)
Bowling: McGrath 10-4-18-2, Dale 10-0-35-0, Moody 10-2-34-2, Symonds 8-0-52-1, Warne 10-0-42-2, Martyn 2-0-12-0

Australia innings

RT Ponting not out	87
+AC Gilchrist c A Flower b Mutendera	28
MG Bevan not out	77
Extras (lb 3, w 6)	9
Total (1 wicket, 39 overs)	201

DNB: DS Lehmann, *SR Waugh, DR Martyn, A Symonds, TM Moody, SK Warne, AC Dale, GD McGrath
Fall: 1-44 (Gilchrist)
Bowling: Rennie 6-1-46-0, Mutendera 6-0-42-1, Blignaut 6-1-25-0, Whittall 8-0-30-0, Brent 10-1-44-0, GW Flower 3-0-11-0

RESULT: AUSTRALIA WON BY NINE WICKETS
UMPIRES: ID ROBINSON AND RB TIFFIN
MAN OF THE MATCH: A FLOWER

GAME 24

AUSTRALIA V NEW ZEALAND
FIFTH ONE-DAY INTERNATIONAL
NAPIER
1 MARCH 2000

The streak. The mere mention of this extraordinary run brings back so many memories. In all, it ran for 13 matches, from our second game in the 1999–2000 World Series to the game I'm highlighting here, played in Napier, the second last of our six one-dayers on our short tour of New Zealand that immediately followed the Australian season. In one sense, I guess there was an element of good fortune in the sequence, because, as I have often said, the nature of one-day cricket is such that it is almost impossible to win a lot of matches in a row. You can win 90 per cent of them, but one time out of 10 someone in the opposing team will do something special, or the pitch or weather conditions or an umpiring decision will work against you. Sometimes, one spectacular catch can turn a game. But in the streak, every win we achieved was well-earned. We played some outstanding cricket, with a myriad of players—Glenn McGrath, Shane Warne, the Waughs, Damien Martyn, Ricky Ponting, Adam Gilchrist, Brett Lee, everyone—in sparkling form. When one bloke had a rare off day, inevitably someone stepped up to take his place. Even the loss of a key player—as happened when Ricky

Ponting was injured during the World Series finals and had to miss the New Zealand trip—could not deflect us from our task.

It wasn't until Steve Waugh became Australia's one-day captain that we really started believing that it was possible to win just about every game we played. I'm not suggesting that we didn't try to win every game in the past, but it was a philosophy within the team (and within all other international one-day teams as well) that you were going to win some and lose some. It was the nature of the game, we were told; no team will ever truly dominate. It was actually the South African teams of 1997 and 1998 who first demonstrated that that theory wasn't necessarily true, and then, after the 1999 World Cup, Australia, under Stephen's captaincy, proved that it was possible to dominate the one-day scene. And we did it for a couple of reasons: one, of course, we were a very good team with some genuinely great players; and two, we recognised that because one-day cricket is a relatively new game there is scope to make improvements and be innovative. If you can marry that innovation with the things that made you successful in the past, then anything is possible.

Before the streak began, the record run in one-day international cricket stood at 11 victories—by the West Indies in 1984–85 and England in 1991–92. Five teams had won 10 in a row, including us Australians, if you count our run from our game against Bangladesh in the 1999 World Cup through to a loss in the final of the Aiwa Cup in Sri Lanka in August of that year. However, that sequence does include the semi-final of the World Cup against South Africa, which, of course, ended in a tie. However, for us it was as good as a win because it got us into the World Cup final, so while I don't think it is appropriate to include it as a run of consecutive victories, it was nevertheless a golden run for the Australian one-day team.

The pressure to sustain the streak never affected us. Our attitude was always that sooner or later our opponents were going to have a good day and knock us off, so we just went out and enjoyed the fact that we were playing good cricket. The spirit in the side was fantastic, everyone was in excellent form, and we fed off each other. Maybe, at the end of the sequence, it worked the other way. We got a bit ahead of ourselves, a bit 'funky', to use a Greg Matthewsism. Rather than continuing to put pressure on ourselves, we started tinkering with our batting and bowling orders, at a time when our opponents were getting more and more desperate to defeat us. Eventually, we had to get beaten.

We realised that while we were playing very well, we could always improve. We wanted to take our cricket to the next level, and saw the potential advantages of trying a few new things. You need to constantly seek a new edge, and maybe one of our new initiatives might have come to something. Damien Martyn was pushed up to the top of the order for our final game, the one that broke the sequence, and responded with a superb century. I know Stephen was keen to switch things around to keep us on our toes, but maybe, in this instance, we got away a bit from focusing on what had won us our status as the best team in the game. Whatever, none of the wins, the loss or the experimenting did us any long-term harm.

Back to Napier. Going into the game, I had more or less been consistently batting at No. 4 since the tour of Zimbabwe that preceded the 1999–2000 Australian season, something I had desired for a while. Obviously, batting 4 gives me an opportunity to face more deliveries, to score a hundred rather than 50; but in the matches before Napier I'd gone OK without ever snaring that big score I craved, my scores in one-day internationals since the move being 25, 77 not out (at No. 3), 31 not out, 41, 2, 15, 77, 83, 11 not out (No. 7), 71, 54, 3 (No. 5), 8 (No. 5), 52 and 37. I knew that I'd batted well but not as well as I could have, and was aware that some observers were pushing for me to be put back to No. 6, on the basis that that was where I gave the team the most value.

Batting at 4 was a fresh challenge. There, you're more likely to come in when the opening bowlers are still on. Sometimes you get to face an almost new ball. I was obliged to play in a different manner from the one which I had been playing in international one-day cricket: for example, I was able to introduce the occasional pull shot into my game; the odd hook, too. I found myself playing more off the back foot, not so much because teams were dropping the ball in short at me, more because in the early overs the quicker bowlers are more liable to go for extra pace and bounce. It was something to get used to, and it probably wasn't until this innings against the Kiwis that I really felt comfortable.

Sticking in my memory today as solidly as the hundred is the catch I dropped during the New Zealand innings. Nathan Astle is an excellent batsman, a key plank in their one-day line-up, not the sort of bloke you want to give too many chances to. But before he scored a run he lobbed a fairly simple catch to me out at mid-off—a simple, knee-high chance—and I put it down. He went on to an outstanding century, and every run he scored cut through me, as they always do after you put down a catch. Making things worse, New Zealand crowds are up there with the worst when it comes to letting you know you've made a blue—or at least they are if it's an Aussie they're aiming their vitriol at. I don't think they've ever really let go of the infamous underarm incident from 1981, when Australian captain Greg Chappell instructed his brother Trevor to bowl a grubber off the last ball of a one-day final in Melbourne, to guarantee a home-town victory. The jibes here in Napier were incessant, rarely funny, often downright abusive, all with the theme that I'd dropped the game.

So I was really pleased to get those runs. It was one of those innings that reminded me why I like to bat, and especially why I like to bat at No. 4. In at 2–34, after Mark Waugh had been dismissed almost immediately and Adam Gilchrist had gone in the seventh over, I was able to control my innings, bat at the pace I wanted to, and help get us home with a comfortable 26 balls to spare. It actually took me 139 balls to reach my hundred, 70 balls to score my second fifty, but never did I feel as though we wouldn't win. Matty Hayden also batted really well, which helped enormously; not coincidentally, it's a lot easier to bat in one-day cricket if your partner is in good touch, keeping the scoreboard ticking over. I was out for 107 from 141 balls, trying for a big finish, which wasn't like me, but I did feel in a mood to celebrate.

However, my pleasure was tempered somewhat after I returned to the dressing room to discover that Damien Martyn had been preferred to me as Ricky Ponting's replacement for the Test series that was to commence after the one-dayers. When the reporters interviewed me after my hundred, their first question was about the catch—'I needed to make amends,' I said with military precision—and then they moved on to the Test selection. Before I could answer, Steve Waugh interrupted, 'The selectors see Bev as a Test player, not just as a one-day player,' he said. 'He was very close to selection for the team.'

It was good to hear that from the skipper, but I knew in my heart that another opportunity to break back into the Test XI had passed me by. Since 1997, it has always seemed that when a spot in the Test team became available my name was on the 'shortlist'. However, the place always went to the other guy, no matter how many runs I might have scored or how often I have proved that I *can* deal with the short ball.

AUSTRALIA V NEW ZEALAND, FIFTH ONE-DAY INTERNATIONAL, 1999–2000
McLEAN PARK, NAPIER
1 MARCH 2000 (50-OVERS MATCH)
TOSS: AUSTRALIA

New Zealand innings
NJ Astle c Gilchrist b Fleming		104
MS Sinclair lbw Fleming		0
*SP Fleming c SR Waugh b Fleming		10
RG Twose b ME Waugh		32
CL Cairns c Warne b McGrath		31
CZ Harris c Hayden b Harvey		15
SB Styris b McGrath		0
+CJ Nevin c Martyn b Warne		11
DL Vettori c Hayden b Fleming		17
SB Doull not out		0
Extras (lb 7, w 12, nb 4)		23
Total (9 wickets, 50 overs)		243

DNB: PJ Wiseman
Fall: 1-2 (Sinclair), 2-26 (Fleming), 3-115 (Twose), 4-177 (Cairns), 5-207 (Harris), 6-208 (Styris), 7-223 (Astle), 8-232 (Nevin), 9-243 (Vettori)
Bowling: McGrath 10-0-61-2, Fleming 8-0-41-4, Harvey 10-0-35-1, Lee 5-0-23-0, Warne 10-2-34-1, ME Waugh 7-0-42-1

Australia innings
+AC Gilchrist c Styris b Cairns		14
ME Waugh c Astle b Cairns		0
ML Hayden st Nevin b Wiseman		57
MG Bevan c Styris b Doull		107
SK Warne c Nevin b Vettori		12
*SR Waugh not out		43
DR Martyn not out		4
Extras (b 3, lb 3, w 2)		8
Total (5 wickets, 45.4 overs)		245

DNB: IJ Harvey, S Lee, DW Fleming, GD McGrath
Fall: 1-1 (ME Waugh), 2-34 (Gilchrist), 3-130 (Hayden), 4-155 (Warne), 5-237 (Bevan)
Bowling: Cairns 8-0-31-2, Doull 7-0-36-1, Styris 6.4-0-46-0, Wiseman 10-0-52-1, Vettori 10-0-47-1, Harris 2-0-17-0, Astle 2-0-10-0

RESULT: AUSTRALIA WON BY FIVE WICKETS
UMPIRES: DB COWIE AND EA WATKIN
MAN OF THE MATCH: MG BEVAN

GAME 25

REST OF THE WORLD XI V ASIA XI
ONE-DAY EXHIBITION MATCH
DHAKA
8 APRIL 2000

Considering the way it all turned out, one of the funny things about this game is that I was only invited to play at the last minute, after other people had pulled out. And I accepted the invitation reluctantly, because we'd just completed a tour of New Zealand, after a gruelling Australian summer, and still had some one-day internationals to play in South Africa before I headed off for a season of county cricket with Sussex. So forgive me if I didn't take it *too* seriously. Four days after this match, I was due to take the field for Australia in a one-day international in Durban. With the other Australians involved in the game—Mark Waugh and Adam Gilchrist—I didn't arrive in Dhaka until around midnight on the night before the match. I can remember the team *not* warming up. Perhaps more than at any other stage in my career, I felt like a performer playing a role, not a cricketer.

Our team was not really suited for the wicket on which we were playing. Phil Tufnell of England was our lone frontline spinner, behind a pace attack of Nantie Hayward (South Africa), Franklyn Rose (West Indies), Andy Caddick (England), Chris Cairns (New Zealand) and Lance

Klusener (South Africa). Hayward, it must be said, was a replacement for South Africa's then captain Hansie Cronje, who had withdrawn from the match as the match-fixing controversy began to explode around him. The story had actually broken the day before, when we were in the air, flying to the game. Like everyone, my initial reaction to this affair was that there was nothing in it but some malicious accusations, but within three days Cronje's career was as good as over. Even today, I remain stunned by the entire match-fixing story; I can look back on games where maybe something might have been going on, when maybe some guys weren't putting in, but I have no firm evidence—for all I know those guys were just having a bad day.

Cairns and Klusener, of course, are all-rounders of the highest order, two of the most damaging hitters in the sport, but it still seemed to me that we were going into the contest with a totally unbalanced attack. I was obliged to bowl a full 10 overs, while our opponents' attack was led by two of the finest spinners in the game, Sri Lanka's Muttiah Muralitharan and Anil Kumble of India.

Not that it really mattered: the game was a promotion, good for cricket in Bangladesh, and entertainment for the estimated full house of 40 000, maybe even 50 000, enthusiastic cricket fans at the ground and the millions watching live on television throughout Asia. The match was sponsored by an Internet company and was conducted as part of a 'cricket week' coordinated by the International Cricket Council. That it came at a time when the game was rife with controversy and gossip heightened its value, so long as we put on a good day/night out.

First up, after Wasim Akram won the toss and opted to bat on that flat, flat wicket, Sachin Tendulkar and Sanath Jayasuriya smashed 49 in a bit more than seven overs. From there, Sachin blazed on to 80 from 77 balls, while his Indian team-mate Sourav Ganguly and Aravinda de Silva of Sri Lanka also scored at a run a ball. The crowd never stopped cheering. When the total reached 250 in the 41st over, I was thinking we'd be chasing upwards of 350, maybe more, so friendly was the wicket and lightning-fast the outfield, but our captain, Mark

Waugh, and his off-breaks came on to stem the flow, and in the end we were happy to restrict them to 9–320.

Mark took Zimbabwe's Neil Johnson out with him, keeping Gilly for the later overs, but Johnson struggled—maybe the fact Wasim started the innings by bowling with a smile and a plastic ball unsettled him— and by the time I came in to join South Africa's Jacques Kallis in the 10th over, the score was only 2–46. Even at this stage our required run-rate was up near seven an over. There was nothing to do but go for it. I'd like to say my tactics were more complex, more scientific, but because the game was an exhibition, because I felt weary rather than inspired, because the task of winning the game seemed so daunting, I just thought, what the heck, go for it.

All through the innings it never looked like we were going to win. Kallis made 27 from 31 balls, but then Cairns, Klusener and Gilchrist— perhaps the three biggest hitters in the world game—were unable to boost the run-rate. Cairns made 8 from 18 deliveries, Klusener 16 from 32, Gilchrist 1 from 7. I was having a good time, teeing off at just about everything, so these guys were happy to play supporting roles, but when Rose was lbw to Abdur Razzaq of Pakistan we needed 125 to win, with 13 overs remaining. That's a fraction more than nine-and-a-half runs per over. Hardly possible.

And Andy Caddick and I nearly got them. I reached my hundred from 85 balls, but even so we still needed more than 50 from the last three overs, 20 from the final six balls. First ball of the last over, we squeezed a bye through to the keeper, and then I hit three fours in a row. The crowd was a unique mixture of frenzied and stunned, in that they'd cheer my shots and then quieten as they realised that their Asian team might not win. Then the buzz would turn into a roar as Abdur Razzaq bowled again, then they'd cheer and quieten as I hit another four. I found it exhilarating. Though the heat and humidity had taken their toll, the thrill of the chase kept me alert. Looking back, the fact that the crowd was so good-humoured added to the pleasure. It was good fun.

With one ball to go we needed five to tie, six to win. But it should have been four to tie, if only Andy hadn't been run out at the bowler's end—coming back for a second off the game's penultimate delivery—by a throw from India's Robin Singh, fielding as a substitute at long-off. Andy had batted so well to this point, but when I saw the replay later he'd taken that run so casually, he should have made it home. All he needed to do was slide his bat, the way you're taught at primary school, but in the excitement he'd started thinking about the final ball too early. We'd added 119 in 77 deliveries.

So when I lofted the final ball to within a metre or two but not quite over the wide long-on boundary, we finished one run short. I'd faced 132 balls, hit 19 fours and five sixes, but best of all, I'd hit the ball as well as I've ever done. My final 91 runs came from 43 balls. The fact that the only obligation was to give the crowd a good show proved what I'd known for a long time—that I bat best when I can relax and just do it.

REST OF THE WORLD XI V ASIA XI, ONE-DAY EXHIBITION MATCH, 1999–2000
BANGABANDHU NATIONAL STADIUM, DHAKA
8 APRIL 2000 (50-OVERS MATCH)
TOSS: ASIA XI

Asia XI innings

ST Jayasuriya c Bevan b Hayward	12
SR Tendulkar c Rose b Tufnell	80
SC Ganguly c Rose b Tufnell	67
PA de Silva c Gilchrist b Bevan	39
A Jadeja c Johnson b Waugh	28
Abdur Razzaq b Waugh	3
+Moin Khan c & b Hayward	34
*Wasim Akram b Hayward	15
A Kumble not out	14
WPUJC Vaas run out	0
M Muralitharan not out	0
Extras (lb 9, w 16, nb 3)	28
Total (9 wickets, 50 overs)	320

Fall: 1-49 (Jayasuriya), 2-163 (Tendulkar), 3-183 (Ganguly), 4-242 (Jadeja), 5-248 (de Silva), 6-248 (Abdur Razzaq), 7-291 (Wasim Akram), 8-314 (Moin Khan), 9-319 (Vaas)
Bowling: Caddick 4-0-27-0, Hayward 7-0-39-3, Rose 6-0-44-0, Cairns 4-0-22-0, Tufnell 9-0-68-2, Klusener 4-0-22-0, Bevan 10-0-61-1, Waugh 6-0-28-2

Rest of the World XI innings

NC Johnson c Jadeja b Wasim Akram	2
*ME Waugh c & b Vaas	28
JH Kallis lbw Kumble	27
MG Bevan not out	185
CL Cairns c & b Muralitharan	8
L Klusener c Jayasuriya b Muralitharan	16
*AC Gilchrist b Abdur Razzaq	1
FA Rose lbw Abdur Razzaq	7
AR Caddick run out	23
M Hayward not out	0
Extras (b 5, lb 13, w 2, nb 2)	22
Total (8 wickets, 50 overs)	319

DNB: PCR Tufnell
Fall: 1-28 (Johnson), 2-46 (Waugh), 3-97 (Kallis), 4-134 (Cairns), 5-180 (Klusener), 6-186 (Gilchrist), 7-196 (Rose), 8-315 (Caddick)
Bowling: Wasim Akram 5-1-27-1, Vaas 10-1-57-1, Abdur Razzaq 10-0-68-2, Kumble 9-0-59-1, Muralitharan 9-1-45-2, Tendulkar 7-0-45-0

RESULT: ASIA XI WON BY ONE RUN
UMPIRES: DL ORCHARD (SA) AND S VENKATARAGHAVAN (IND)
MAN OF THE MATCH: MG BEVAN

GAME 26

AUSTRALIA V SOUTH AFRICA
FIRST INDOOR ONE-DAY INTERNATIONAL
COLONIAL STADIUM, MELBOURNE
16 AUGUST 2000

This historic match was played amid the continuing match-fixing controversy, which had been simmering away, sometimes sensationally boiling over, as enquiries were conducted in Pakistan, India and South Africa. Some of the revelations were astonishing, and among the most surprised people were the many players who had remained oblivious to the scheming and skullduggery that had taken place. I was aware, as we all were, that from time to time some guys had received approaches from shady characters, and had lived through the controversies that had touched the Australian side, most notably the incidents involving Salim Malik, Shane Warne, Tim May and Mark Waugh in Pakistan in 1994, and then the aftermath of the decision to keep secret the fact that Shane and Mark had been fined after providing information to an Indian bookmaker. But I was still amazed by the extent to which match-fixing, under-the-table payments and illegal bookmakers had apparently infiltrated the game.

One consequence of all this was that in the lead-up to the historic one-day 'indoor' series against South Africa in August 2000, the members of both teams were all extremely conscious that we had an important role to play in starting the process of rebuilding the game's image. This was a responsibility players from every team carried, and as I write this now, the best part of two years later, I can't help thinking that the job hasn't been done too badly. The match-fixing scandal could have truly wrecked the game, and while I am not so naïve as to think that the problem has been totally eradicated, the game has retained its status as one of the world's most notable sports, which to me is a genuine achievement.

These indoor games were a real success. Whether they represented an exciting new innovation for cricket in Australia and beyond or simply a novel one-off, no one could be sure, but the pitches—specially grown in a glasshouse and then implanted into the Colonial Stadium in the middle of winter—were outstanding, the lights worked well, the roof successfully kept the worst of Melbourne's greyest months outside, and the fans, albeit many wearing their football scarves and beanies, turned up in their thousands. The ratings on television were reasonable, and some of the cricket was excellent. The series itself finished level: one win each with the middle game tied.

So who was the first batsman to score a one-day international hundred indoors? Michael Bevan is the correct answer, a feat I achieved in this first match. I made it by a single delivery—off the next ball Steve Waugh reached his hundred as we added 218 in 35.1 overs for the fourth wicket. As always I enjoyed batting with the captain, especially the way we worked between the wickets, taking every single possible, turning ones into twos, constantly encouraging each other. After I was dismissed, Shane Lee came out and hit the first six in an indoor one-day international, and the second, and we ended up with 5–295, not a bad total for a team that was first up from a spell. South Africa, in reply, came up 94 runs short; it was a very satisfying victory.

The fact that I had been playing well for Sussex through the northern hemisphere summer certainly helped me. I had scored hundreds in four of my previous six games in England, so my form at Colonial was really a carryover of that.

The change rooms were world class, everything was terrific; the only problem I could find with the entire presentation was the soft, spongy playing surface, which was apparently a result of the way the stadium was constructed, with its sloping grandstand roof, and also of the fact that the roof was often closed. The sun rarely shone on the outfield, so it was not likely to be baked hard. After that first match, where I scored a hundred and then ran around the outfield for 50 overs, I could not move my body for the next two games. I felt as if I'd run up and down the soft sand of a beach for a week, and my hamstrings, quadriceps, groin and hips were very sore. I made only 3 in game two, coming at No. 8, and then struggled to 33 in the decider, finally getting myself run out in a manner I probably wouldn't have done if my body had been operating on all cylinders.

Still, the three matches were a success. The attendance figures were: 25 785, then 35 724, then 32 769, at a time when we were competing for attention with the Australian Football League, the National Rugby League, the Wallabies, the lead-up to the Olympics, all sorts of things. Throughout, the atmosphere was vibrant, though I couldn't help wondering why they hadn't turned the heaters on; it was as chilly inside as it was out, in the middle of winter.

Of course, one of the criticisms of one-day cricket is that there is too much of it, that the goose that provided cricket with this wonderful source of gold is being plucked too often. Indeed, this issue became a feature of the match-fixing investigations, with strong suggestions that one of the things that led the corrupt players down their path to ruin was the fact that too many one-day internationals were 'meaningless'. If the games didn't matter, so the argument went, why not make some easy cash out of them. I could understand the rationale behind this argument, but it didn't sit well with the philosophy of the Australian squad, because we play every game as if it is our last.

The fact that we were playing under a roof in Melbourne in August just reflected the fact that the game is still evolving. Test cricket is nearly 130 years old, one-day cricket is just past 30. The game has only been an entertainment vehicle, as well as a sport, since World Series Cricket became a reality, back in the late 1970s. Even today, not everyone realises that there is a real art to the one-day game. For a long time, many people—including some very notable players and commentators—liked to argue that one-day cricket brought the standard of all the teams closer together, as if the game's makeup somehow stifled talent. When Sri Lanka won the World Cup in 1996, some liked to say that this proved that ordinary teams could beat the better sides. This was total nonsense—if only they'd stopped to see how well the Sri Lankans played the one-day game, how clever and innovative their tactics were. A lot of teams didn't know how to play one-day cricket, but Sri Lanka did. Since then, I think that Australia has worked it out and the South Africans have worked it out, both teams have striven to be excellent, and we win most of our matches. The clashes between the two teams are always super-competitive, whether they are played in summer or winter, home or away, outdoors or indoors.

I'm sure one-day international cricket will keep evolving. My hope is that the fact that it is an entertainment vehicle and the fact that it makes a lot of money for the cricket authorities will never overwhelm the fact that players treat the game seriously, that it's a significant part of many guys' careers, and that it needs to retain its competitive element. If it becomes *pure* entertainment, without the passion that comes with meaningful contests, then it will be competing on level terms with other forms of entertainment, such as movies, soap operas and the like. And we all know what happens to soap operas that don't rate. It's important to keep the game growing, to keep it exciting, but it has to matter to the people who play it and the people who follow it. It has to remain a sport.

This became an issue nearly two years after the first indoor matches, when we returned to Melbourne to play another indoor series, with a match at the Gabba thrown in after two at Colonial Stadium. The games were competitive on the field, but much-criticised off it, as we struggled for media exposure when up against a number of other major sporting events, most notably the soccer World Cup, plus the Australian Football, rugby league's State of Origin, the US Open golf, rugby union Tests, the French Open tennis, you name it. Still, though the crowds were well down on 2000, the ratings were OK, especially on the sub-continent, and the cricket was competitive, with Pakistan winning the deciding third game. The outfield was much better, too, I have to say. My only criticism is that the timing of the series could have been better—I think the fans and the players would have preferred the matches to have been closer to the start of the Australian season, in August, as they were in 2000, rather than June, in 2002.

The question I was most often asked during the latter series was this: 'Are you enjoying it?' And the answer is not a simple yes or no. On the day, yes, I enjoyed it—I love cricket, love matching my skills with the best in the game, love trying to get the best out of myself; these are the major reasons I play the game. However, because I play so much cricket these days—to a large degree by my own choice, I must stress—sometimes I could do without the grind that comes with all these matches, the travel, the hotel rooms, the occasional not-quite-knowing-in-what-city-or-town-I've-woken-up-in feeling. Still, that's a small price to pay for all the good times. And I know I'd rather be playing for Australia at any venue at any time than watching someone else play in my place.

AUSTRALIA V SOUTH AFRICA, FIRST INDOOR ONE-DAY INTERNATIONAL, 2000
COLONIAL STADIUM, MELBOURNE
16 AUGUST 2000 (50-OVERS MATCH)
TOSS: SOUTH AFRICA

Australia innings

+AC Gilchrist run out	1
ME Waugh c Hayward b Telemachus	17
RT Ponting c Rhodes b Telemachus	16
MG Bevan c Kallis b Pollock	106
*SR Waugh not out	114
S Lee c Cullinan b Kallis	28
IJ Harvey not out	1
Extras (b 2, lb 2, w 3, nb 5)	12
Total (5 wickets, 50 overs)	295

DNB: DR Martyn, SK Warne, B Lee, GD McGrath
Fall: 1-1 (Gilchrist), 2-32 (Ponting), 3-37 (ME Waugh), 4-259 (Bevan), 5-289 (S Lee)
Bowling: Pollock 10-0-46-1, Telemachus 10-1-54-2, Kallis 10-0-74-1, Hayward 6-0-45-0, Klusener 8-0-43-0, Hall 6-0-29-0

South Africa innings

G Kirsten st Gilchrist b Warne	43
AJ Hall c Gilchrist b Harvey	11
JH Kallis lbw Harvey	42
DJ Cullinan b Harvey	29
JN Rhodes c Martyn b Warne	16
L Klusener not out	25
ND McKenzie b S Lee	22
+MV Boucher c Bevan b S Lee	6
*SM Pollock not out	4
Extras (lb 2, w 1)	3
Total (7 wickets, 50 overs)	201

DNB: M Hayward, R Telemachus
Fall: 1-37 (Hall), 2-70 (Kirsten), 3-124 (Cullinan), 4-137 (Kallis), 5-148 (Rhodes), 6-179 (McKenzie), 7-189 (Boucher)
Bowling: McGrath 10-2-28-0, B Lee 10-0-51-0, Harvey 10-0-41-3, S Lee 10-0-41-2, Warne 10-0-38-2

RESULT: AUSTRALIA WON BY 94 RUNS
UMPIRES: DB HAIR AND SJA TAUFEL
MAN OF THE MATCH: SR WAUGH

GAME 27

NEW SOUTH WALES V WESTERN AUSTRALIA
MERCANTILE MUTUAL CUP FINAL
WACA GROUND, PERTH
25 FEBRUARY 2001

The hundred I managed in this game is right up there on my list of favourite innings. For a couple of reasons. One, until this dig I'd never made a hundred in domestic one-day cricket in Australia. Two, before the game, the Western Australians had been talking up the fact that they were going to bowl short to me, to give it to me. I'd been facing short balls for the previous three or four years and played them all pretty well, yet they brought the old chestnut out of the cupboard. I guess they saw mine as a crucial wicket. Whether WA captain Tom Moody was trying to rev up some interest in the game, use a bit of gamesmanship or outlining a specific strategy, I don't know, but I was irked by the lack of respect. Whatever the logic was behind their public pronouncements, all it did was fire me up—I turned around and said, 'Right, if they're going to bowl short, I want to take it to them too, I'll take them on'. The hook and pull are shots I can play, but don't often play—but I was going to play them here.

The WA captain was helped by the rules governing the Mercantile Mutual Cup, Australia's domestic one-day competition. Whereas bouncers—that is, as far as one-day cricket is concerned, a delivery that goes past the batsman at a height between his shoulder and head—were prohibited in international one-day cricket at this time (this was subsequently changed by the International Cricket Council in September 2001, in time for the 2001–02 VB Series), in these matches you could bowl one an over.

On the morning of the final, I found myself as anxious as I'd been for a long time before a game. But I made this work to my advantage. After they batted very well to reach 7–272, Tom Moody and Mike Hussey both scoring excellent half-centuries, I knew my time had come.

The fact that they scored such a big total helped me, too, because I'd have been obliged to take them on anyway, purely because of the run-rate required and the fact that I was the Blues' senior batsman. I was in at No. 3, at 1–14 in the fourth over, and working on the principle of one-day batting that I've always believed in—that you look for boundaries in the first 15 overs and then work the gaps as the fieldsmen are allowed out of the fielding circles. Against the WA bowlers here, I was determined to maintain at least a run-a-ball rate in the early overs, so when they fired them in short I did go after them. And I kept going for my big shots longer here than I would have in a one-day international, because in this competition another rule modification stated that between overs 16 and 30 they could have only three men outside the fielding circles. Not until over 31 could five men go back on the boundary, and by then I was in total control. As I said, I would have batted hard even if they hadn't mouthed off before the game, but the fact that they'd done so made the boundaries I struck all the sweeter. I was very, very happy with the way I hit them. It was a big innings for me, made in a crunch game on a bouncy wicket, very satisfying.

So many aspects of the innings were good for me, but none more so than the fact that I had to come out of my 'comfort zone' to succeed. It's always pleasing when you don't play to your strengths but still do well. In the end, I was able to put the pressure back on them. They had a good pace attack—Brad Williams, Jo Angel, Duncan Spencer and Brendon Julian—but having talked their short balls up before the game, and then seen their strategy come unstuck during the early overs, they struggled while we prospered. Spencer, once rated the fastest bowler in the land, had reputedly been brought into the WA team specifically to target me, but by the time he came on I was well established, 55 not out, in the 21st over. He started with three wides in his second over and, though he did take two wickets, was never really a factor.

When I hit Kade Harvey away for my 14th boundary—the winning runs—with 10 balls still available, I was 135 not out, my highest innings in domestic or international one-day cricket, made from 137 balls. After the initial onslaught I was able to pick them off as it suited me to get us home. My first 50 actually came from 44 balls, the 100 from 119. It was the first time NSW had won the domestic one-day competition since 1993–94.

Australia's domestic one-day cricket has always intrigued me. In some ways it is hard to compare our one-day domestic game to the cricket played in the international arena, because some of the rules in our local competition are different. Australia has pioneered some rule changes, all in their way worthy and many of them popular with fans and players alike, but they do alter the way the game is played.

In the Mercantile Mutual Cup, each team is made up of 12 players, though only 11 can bat and only 11 can field at any one time. Thus, most teams can take an extra bowler in, which takes away the chance to get at the 'fifth' bowler, who in international one-day cricket is often a part-timer. In that 2000–01 final, Duncan Spencer (a specialist quick) was selected as WA's fifth bowler. We also had bonus points to reward teams that won decisively—an innovation used with, shall we say, mixed success in the 2001–02 VB Series—and, of course, there are the rules relating to the fielding circles and the bouncer rule.

Bowling short ones in one-day cricket can be something of a double-edged sword. The embargo on them in international one-dayers that existed for many years allowed batsmen to get more onto the front foot, and also meant that captains were less inclined to have fieldsmen out on the backward-point and backward-square boundaries. Instead, those fieldsmen would be placed in front of square. If a short one can be bowled, it changes the psyche of the batsman as well as the bowler. For the bowler, do you throw it in early or keep it until late in the over? For the batsman, the question is, do I wait for the bumper and then hook at it? If a fieldsman is out on the fence, that adds to the equation, and the theatre. And as the WA bowlers found when they attacked me in this final, if a batsman does go for the hook and the pull, and the assault comes off and the runs flow, it can set the mood by catapulting the batsman into a long, attacking innings.

Later in 2001, in a Pura Cup match against WA at the Sydney Cricket Ground, I became the leading run-scorer for the state in first-class cricket. This was a bit ironic, given that I'm originally from the ACT. I look upon this landmark with mixed feelings. I am grateful for the opportunities NSW cricket has given me, and appreciate that making more runs for the Blues than legendary players such as Trumper, Kippax, Morris, Walters and the Waughs is an achievement. But I know, too, that the fact that I've scored so many runs in Shield cricket means that I haven't played very often for Australia, something I share with other leading run-makers in domestic cricket in recent seasons—men such as David Hookes, Jamie Siddons and Darren Lehmann.

Playing for NSW has been a major part of my life. For the first five years, we were one of the best sides going around. That was great to be part of. The last five years, in contrast, have been a bit of a struggle, but one thing that has never changed is that we have continued to produce Test cricketers. You can pick a pretty fair XI out of Blues who have worn the baggy green since I made my international debut in 1994: Mark Taylor, Michael Slater, Mark Waugh, Steve Waugh, Michael Bevan, Phil Emery, Gavin Robertson, Simon Cook, Stuart MacGill, Brett Lee and Glenn McGrath. As well, guys such as Anthony Stuart, Nathan Bracken, Shane Lee and Brad Haddin have played one-day international cricket in the past eight years.

As I explained earlier in this book, when I first came into the side, the NSW team contained passionate senior Blues such as Mike Whitney, Greg Matthews and Geoff Lawson, who really made the younger guys aware of the traditions of NSW cricket, what we were part of. That hasn't happened as much in recent years, perhaps because the international players nowadays can be away from the domestic scene almost totally, or at least enough of the time to make it hard for them to come back and force themselves on the team psyche. The sheer number of international cricket matches these days can make it very difficult for teams with a number of Test and one-day international players, which might help explain why the dominant states in Australian domestic cricket in the past few years have been those who are not as heavily involved at the international level.

I can admit that when I first started playing top-class cricket, the game's traditions didn't mean that much to me. But the longer I have played, the more ups and downs I have had, and the more major events that I have been a part of or close to, the more I have come to realise that I am a part of cricket history, however small my contribution might have been. And I've also come to appreciate the skill involved in the notable feats of former champions, and the importance of their achievements.

I finished that 2001–02 Australian first-class season the second Australian on the batting averages list (of those to score at least 300 runs, behind Matty Hayden), and throughout I felt I hit the ball as well as I ever had. As a batsman, I felt I was in control. It was the best I've felt in a long time. But I still wasn't picked in the Test squad for the South African tour; instead the selectors went for Darren Lehmann as the seventh batsman.

For me, while missing out was a disappointment, the fact that Darren was chosen was a positive. For the past couple of seasons the selectors have been backing Simon Katich as that extra batsman, on the basis, no doubt, that he was the most promising young batsman in the country. The fact that they picked Boof for South Africa came as a surprise, not because of his form but because he was the 'other' side of 30 years of age, so the fact that they turned to him means that there is no reason for me to dismiss the possibility of being chosen again.

NEW SOUTH WALES V WESTERN AUSTRALIA, MERCANTILE MUTUAL CUP FINAL, 2000–01
WACA GROUND, PERTH
25 FEBRUARY 2001 (50-OVERS MATCH) ▲
TOSS: WESTERN AUSTRALIA

Western Australia innings
*TM Moody c Higgs b MacGill	78
+RJ Campbell c Higgs b Bracken	10
SM Katich c Haddin b Bracken	4
MW Goodwin c Haddin b Lee	38
BP Julian b Lee	14
MEK Hussey not out	84
MJ North b Thompson	14
GB Hogg c Haddin b Bradstreet	1
KM Harvey not out	20
Extras (b 1, lb 5, w 2, nb 1)	9
Total (7 wickets, 50 overs)	272

DNB: DJ Spencer, J Angel, BA Williams
Fall: 1-23 (Campbell), 2-30 (Katich), 3-133 (Moody), 4-139 (Goodwin), 5-152 (Julian), 6-182 (North), 7-185 (Hogg)
Bowling: Bracken 10-2-43-2, Clark 9-0-63-0, Nash 5-0-26-0, Lee 10-1-39-2, MacGill 8-1-46-1, Bradstreet 4-0-24-1, Thompson 4-0-25-1

New South Wales innings
MJ Clarke c Campbell b Spencer	57
+BJ Haddin c Spencer b Williams	8
MG Bevan not out	135
*S Lee c Hussey b Spencer	6
MA Higgs c Moody b Angel	29
GC Rummans not out	30
Extras (lb 4, w 5, nb 2)	11
Total (4 wickets, 48.2 overs)	276

DNB: SM Thompson, SD Bradstreet, DA Nash, SCG MacGill, NW Bracken, SR Clark
Fall: 1-14 (Haddin), 2-140 (Clarke), 3-146 (Lee), 4-207 (Higgs)
Bowling: Angel 10-0-40-1, Williams 9-1-44-1, Julian 5-0-23-0, Moody 5-1-29-0, Spencer 7-0-57-2, Harvey 5.2-0-32-0, Hogg 7-0-47-0

RESULT: NEW SOUTH WALES WON BY SIX WICKETS
UMPIRES: DB HAIR AND DJ HARPER
MAN OF THE MATCH: MG BEVAN

▲ Players per side: 12 (11 bat, 11 field)

GAME 28

The Test series that preceded this one-day series was one of the greatest ever staged, including an astonishing fightback by the Indians in the second Test and a couple of thrilling finishes. Such was the renown of these Tests, the one-day series has been largely forgotten, which is unfortunate because it too evolved into a classic contest.

It wouldn't have surprised me if our Test guys had been despondent after losing the third Test in pretty heartbreaking circumstances. Having lost the second Test despite making India follow-on, they'd been obliged to back up straightaway in the deciding match, and only lost after a terrific battle that came down to the final two wickets of the Indian second innings. I know it had been a great ambition of the guys to win a series in India, something no Australian side has done since 1969–70, but they rebounded really quickly, a tribute to the spirit Steve Waugh and John Buchanan have built across both Australian squads.

The tour represented a real turning point for Matthew Hayden. Matty had enjoyed a sensational Test series, scoring 549 runs at 109.80, including a double century, a century and two fifties, so impressive that the selectors opted to keep him on for the one-dayers. And his fantastic form continued, to the point that by the end of the series Australia had three of the finest opening batsmen in the one-day game: Haydos, Mark Waugh and Adam Gilchrist.

One thing that set these one-day games apart was the fact that the matches were played on pitches that really turned. From my previous experience, when you go to the sub-continent, the wickets for the three-, four- and five-day games turn appreciably but the one-dayers are generally true; they might turn a bit but they're good tracks for one-day cricket. But in this series, for a couple of matches at least, the wickets spun big-time from the first over, which had us thinking that perhaps the authorities were tailoring things to suit their new star, the off-spinner Harbhajan Singh, who had taken 32 wickets in the three Tests. We took this as an extra challenge, and had the better of the exchanges with Harbhajan through the one-day series.

Against the best spinners in the game, in most situations, dependent on field settings, I believe the key to scoring runs at a reasonable rate is to find ways to rotate the strike. If you get pinned down against blokes such as Warne, Muralitharan, Kumble or Pakistan's Saqlain Mushtaq, then you're in trouble, but that's not just true in one-day cricket. If they tie you down, they'll get you in the end. Who's the toughest spinner I've faced in one-day cricket? The bloke I've found hardest to get away has been Saqlain, a bit more awkward than Murali, a bit harder to read, both in the way he spins the ball and his ability to vary his pace. Neither are conventional off-spinners, both are great bowlers. Warney's better than either of them, I reckon, but luckily I don't have to bat against him.

This series in India fluctuated wildly; the home team would win comfortably, to much rejoicing, then we'd prevail just as easily, and it all came down to this final game, in the coastal town of Margao. The track was slow, built on a base of red clay, and it turned a lot, too. The key wicket, we thought initially, was Sachin Tendulkar, and we dismissed him quickly, a caught-behind to remember for our rookie left-arm quick Nathan Bracken. There's usually an advantage of around 30 runs if you get Sachin early, but on this occasion VVS Laxman played so well Sachin's wicket might not have made as much difference as usual. Normally in India I would say that 220 was very gettable, but as the track seemed to be getting lower and slower by the over, that was the kind of modest target we had in mind. But with Laxman's effort and Sourav Ganguly's support, India reached 265, leaving us up against it.

Fortunately Hayden and Gilchrist got us off to a terrific start, smashing 70 from the first 10 overs. Gilly went on to 76 from 60 deliveries (after reaching his fifty from just 28 balls, with nine fours and a six), but the Indian spinners came on and slowed things down, to the point that when Ian Harvey joined me in the middle we required 68 from 10.5 overs, pretty much a run a ball, to win the series. At first glance, it seemed that Steve Waugh (17 from 30 balls) and I (it took me 79 balls to reach my fifty, with just two fours) had gone too slowly, but in fact the rapid start at the top of the order had allowed Tugga and me to bat at our pace, and set up a platform for our final assault.

I've always thought that 'Harvs' was an extremely talented all-round cricketer, a terrific stroke-maker who can play every shot, a guy with plenty to offer in one-day cricket. He's a guy who's brave enough to try things in pressure situations, and often ice cool at the death. I've seen him bowl yorker after yorker at the end of an innings, varying his pace cleverly, frustrating batsmen who were thinking fours but going nowhere. I've heard people call him an underrated cricketer, but he's not underrated within the Australian team.

Harvs took a few balls to settle himself in, and then the two of us set about getting the runs that mattered. At the end of my innings I was going at a run a ball, and Harvs matched me as we went on to win the game with two full overs to spare. In the media conference afterwards I described the knock as 'certainly one of my best ever'. It was an important victory; it would have been tough mentally on the boys to have lost both the Test and one-day series on this tour by narrow margins. Instead, we had something very positive to take out of our time in India, which set us up for what was to become another highly successful Ashes tour.

AUSTRALIA V INDIA, FIFTH ONE-DAY INTERNATIONAL, 2000–01
NEHRU STADIUM, MARGAO
6 APRIL 2001 (50-OVERS MATCH)
TOSS: INDIA

India innings
*SC Ganguly c Ponting b McGrath	74
SR Tendulkar c Gilchrist b Bracken	12
VVS Laxman c Gilchrist b Harvey	101
R Dravid c Waugh b Symonds	31
HK Badani b Harvey	7
Yuvraj Singh run out	19
+V Dahiya not out	15
Z Khan not out	0
Extras (lb 3, w 3)	6
Total (6 wickets, 50 overs)	265

DNB: AB Agarkar, Harbhajan Singh, J Srinath
Fall: 1-16 (Tendulkar), 2-121 (Ganguly), 3-218 (Dravid), 4-230 (Laxman), 5-230 (Badani), 6-262 (Yuvraj Singh)
Bowling: McGrath 8-0-37-1, Bracken 10-1-37-1, Harvey 10-1-49-2, Warne 8-0-62-0, Symonds 8-0-40-1, Lehmann 6-0-37-0

Australia innings
ML Hayden c Ganguly b Srinath	36
+AC Gilchrist b Tendulkar	76
RT Ponting c Dahiya b Srinath	4
MG Bevan not out	87
*SR Waugh c Agarkar b Tendulkar	17
DS Lehmann c Yuvraj Singh b Tendulkar	1
A Symonds c Badani b Srinath	7
IJ Harvey not out	25
Extras (b 4, lb 9, w 1, nb 2)	16
Total (6 wickets, 48 overs)	269

DNB: SK Warne, GD McGrath, NW Bracken
Fall: 1-70 (Hayden), 2-74 (Ponting), 3-142 (Gilchrist), 4-187 (Waugh), 5-195 (Lehmann), 6-202 (Symonds)
Bowling: Srinath 10-1-62-3, Khan 9-0-43-0, Agarkar 6-0-45-0, Harbhajan Singh 10-0-55-0, Tendulkar 10-0-35-3, Yuvraj Singh 3-0-16-0

RESULT: AUSTRALIA WON BY FOUR WICKETS
UMPIRES: F GOMES AND SK POREL
MAN OF THE MATCH: MG BEVAN

GAME 29

Imagine the scene. You're an Australian cricketer, part of a team that has just dominated an important match at the home of cricket, Lord's. After the game has been decisively won, you shake hands with your vanquished opponents, then walk back through the famous Long Room and up to your dressing room, but only briefly, because then you go out with your animated team-mates onto the equally famous balcony for the presentations. You don your sponsor's cap, push through to a reasonably obscure spot, about three-quarters of the way along the line, just between Punter and Junior will do. You look out over the masses of people congregating on the outfield below, the first speech begins . . .

And then, THUMP!!, you cop a full can of beer on the side of the head.

It probably took me around 20 seconds to realise what had happened. Initially, I had no idea. I thought someone must have punched me, maybe someone had thrown a cricket ball at me. I remember, as a young kid, being hit when someone threw a cricket ball at my face and it was the same feeling. And then someone shouted out that they had seen a can flying my way and I looked down and saw the sponsor's product lying on the ground and knew what had transpired. Which wrecked what had been a really good day, a win as decisive as our World Cup final victory of two years before, achieved at the same venue against the same opponents.

To be honest, I didn't know what to think at the time and I'm still not sure what to think about the incident today. I just can't understand why anyone would want to do that, indiscriminately fling a full can in among the players. The intention had to have been to hurt someone, but the can-thrower didn't care whom he hurt, or how badly. In the end, I was lucky not to be seriously injured, because the soft side of the missile struck me on the soft part of the cheek. Had it hit me on my cheekbone or jaw, or if I'd been hit by the can's hard edge, I could easily have broken a bone and/or lost some teeth. Who knows how bad the damage might have been. I mean, for everyone—players and fans— it's just a game, a form of entertainment, whether your team is winning or losing; everyone should be involved to enjoy themselves. At least that's what I think.

At the media conference afterwards, Steve Waugh was scathing about the incident and the whole question of crowd behaviour. 'Someone will get killed,' Stephen said, arguing for greater protection of players, 'there's no doubt about it. Maybe we've reached the lowest point with the spectators, and something will be done and it will be recognised that there are problems. Precautions have got to be taken. It might be plastic cups instead of bottles and cans in future.'

Ricky Ponting reminded me later how a throwaway line of his might have saved me from serious damage. Just before I was clobbered, Punter pointed to our left on the balcony and said to me, 'Look at the camera'. I turned to my left instinctively, and the can hit me on the right cheek. Otherwise, I might have copped it nose first.

As soon as he realised what had happened to me, Stephen said, 'We're out of here'. The rest of the presentation ceremony was held inside.

Back in the rooms, I was flat on my back, nursing a huge icepack on my right cheek that kept the swelling down, to the point that by the following day you could hardly see a mark. A police report was filed and that was it. I was told much later that they found the bloke who threw the can, but I have no idea if he was punished in any way for the offence, or what his background or motivation were.

The tournament itself was a beauty for Australia, but a quiet one for me. I scored 56 not out in our first-up win over Pakistan in Cardiff, part of a dominant display in which we bowled and fielded well to keep our opponents to 257 and then batted superbly to pass that total with seven wickets and more than four overs to spare. The team put on a similar performance to beat England in Bristol, thrashed the Poms at Old Trafford and The Oval, but lost to Pakistan in a high-scoring game at Trent Bridge. My only significant contribution with the bat was a 37 in Manchester, my other efforts being 5 and 4 not out. I missed the first game against England, due to the 'rotation' system the team hierarchy had instigated, and didn't bat in the final. Throughout, we faced a string of problems with crowd control; Stephen seemed to be forever complaining about crowd invasions and objects being thrown onto the field from the crowds, and the officials seemed to be forever offering token solutions or simply failing to respond at all. Given this, maybe it wasn't such a surprise that a player was struck in the manner I was after the final. It was a pity this controversy at Lord's over-shadowed the fact that we played such good cricket throughout the tournament.

I couldn't help but think about the difference between our approach and that of, arguably, our chief rivals of recent times, the South Africans. Their approach is to be very clinical, very thorough, in the way they play one-day cricket, but I believe they have erred too often on the side of caution. Their strategy has been to build up pressure by restricting their opponent's scoring; that's how they get their wickets.

In contrast, Australian teams of the past few seasons, armed as they have been with bowlers such as Glenn McGrath, Shane Warne, Jason Gillespie and Brett Lee, have been more aggressive. This approach was never more evident than in this series in England, especially in the game at Old Trafford when McGrath and Gillespie were charging in at the Poms supported by three slips, two gullies and no third man. Part of our thinking was to gain a psychological advantage over our hosts that would last for the rest of the tour, and when England were bowled out for 86 it seemed we had achieved this aim. But another part of our thinking was to test out the theory that there is a place in one-day cricket for all-out attack when you're bowling, provided you have the bowlers to do so and the conditions and match situation justify such an onslaught. Batsmen such as Adam Gilchrist, Sachin Tendulkar and Sanath Jayasiruya have demonstrated how such aggression can pay dividends for top-class batsmen; at Old Trafford, when Gillespie and McGrath went through the top of the English order, we showed that it can work for bowlers as well.

We are an aggressive team by nature, but never before had we taken this mind-set as far as having so many men in the slip cordon. This aggression has always been reflected in our fielding, which was excellent when I first came into the team, back in 1994, but is even better now. This improvement has not come about because we work any harder these days. I don't think we do—I put it down to nothing more complicated than natural evolution. Just as success can breed success, so can the class of one player in the field inspire brilliance in others. Eventually, superb fielding efforts can become commonplace, so that, for example, when Allan Border started hitting the stumps consistently with throws from midwicket he was setting an example that guys such as Ricky Ponting, Jonty Rhodes, Damien Martyn and others have followed. It's definitely riskier to take a quick single these days than it was a decade ago.

When I first came into the Australian set-up, Bob Simpson was coach. From what I understand, when Bob became coach in the mid-1980s he was the guy who first had the Australian players working overtime on their fielding skills. As the Australian team improved, winning the 1987 World Cup as it did so, it became universally accepted that extensive fielding practice needed to be a big part of a team's preparation. Teams that didn't work hard on their fielding skills fell behind. Today, John Buchanan works us just as hard, but no harder than did Bob Simpson, though he has added more variety to our fielding drills. And you do need that variety these days, if only to keep us fresh because we play so much cricket. Keeping your troops stimulated is part of a coach's role in the 21st century.

Another innovation that became an issue around this time, and on into the 2001–02 Australian season, was the 'rotation system'. Through all the criticism of this policy, which might even have played a part in Steve Waugh losing the one-day captaincy in early 2002, I wondered whether the people who liked to bag it really stopped to appreciate what the concept was trying to achieve. And what it did achieve. The negative, of course, is that rotating excellent players in and out of the team meant that we didn't always put onto the paddock what appeared on paper to be our top XI. Against that, it gave everyone in the squad an opportunity, and also meant that more than just 11 or 12 guys had the experience of playing one-day cricket at the highest level. Inevitably, by the time the World Cup—the game's most prestigious one-day tournament—comes along, you need to have a squad of players you know will be able to deliver in the clutch situations. We also took the chance to rest key players, primarily our fast bowlers, rather than exposing them to the grind and physical stress of playing every day. Careers can be extended this way. Through the rotation system, guys such as Damien Martyn and Matthew Hayden emerged as genuine one-day stars, when under a more rigid selection policy they might never have had an opportunity. And the rotation concept went beyond the selection table, in that players were given a go in various places in the batting order, and bowled at different times in our opponents' innings. Thus we saw how good Ian Harvey can be in the final overs, discovered that Marto and Darren Lehmann can open the batting, while I was given an extended run at No. 4. Maybe we lost a couple of games because of the rotation system, but I'm sure the positives outweighed the negatives.

Before arriving in England in 2001, we experienced something that I found extremely moving. Through the efforts of Steve Waugh, Australian Cricket Board officials and the Australian Army, we were given the opportunity to go to Gallipoli on the way to England. Now I'm not into war history, had never really stopped to think about the significance of World War I battle theatres such as Gallipoli or the fields in France, so when I was told we were going, I wasn't too sure how I'd react. It certainly wasn't something that I've always wanted to do. Yet I left Gallipoli completely in awe of what happened to the Australians who fought there, totally stunned by the awful predicament they faced. More than anything, it gave me a sense of wonder: about what they went through and how their lives and deaths were so controlled by senior officers. It was an abuse of power, no doubt, to send uncomplicated, brave men to their deaths in that way.

As the stories of the battles and the casualties were explained to us, I was given a sense of perspective on what I do for a living, and a reminder of how lucky I am. When my wife and I started a family, I thought I might sit back and say to myself, 'Maybe cricket doesn't matter'. But I didn't, because it does matter, it matters a lot. But my kids did give me a sense of perspective, and still do. The Gallipoli experience was the same. Cricket is important to me, I want to do well at it, but it's not the only thing, the be-all and end-all. I'm a better cricketer and better person for knowing that.

AUSTRALIA V PAKISTAN, NATWEST SERIES ONE-DAY FINAL, 2001
LORD'S, LONDON
23 JUNE 2001 (50-OVERS MATCH)
TOSS: PAKISTAN

Pakistan innings

Saeed Anwar c Bevan b Harvey	27
Saleem Elahi c Gilchrist b McGrath	10
Yousuf Youhana run out	11
Inzamam-ul-Haq lbw Warne	23
Younis Khan c Warne b Lee	0
Abdur Razzaq c Warne b Lee	24
+Rashid Latif b Warne	23
Azhar Mahmood b Warne	1
Wasim Akram b Gillespie	17
*Waqar Younis lbw Harvey	0
Saqlain Mushtaq not out	0
Extras (b 2, lb 3, w 8, nb 3)	16
Total (all out, 42.3 overs)	152

Fall: 1-28 (Saleem Elahi), 2-47 (Saeed Anwar), 3-60 (Yousuf Youhana), 4-60 (Younis Khan), 5-92 (Abdur Razzaq), 6-102 (Inzamam-ul-Haq), 7-110 (Azhar Mahmood), 8-151 (Rashid Latif), 9-152 (Wasim Akram), 10-152 (Waqar Younis)
Bowling: McGrath 10-2-28-1, Gillespie 7-1-25-1, Harvey 7.3-0-18-2, Lee 8-1-20-2, Warne 10-0-56-3

Australia innings

+AC Gilchrist not out	76
ME Waugh run out	36
RT Ponting not out	35
Extras (lb 1, w 8)	9
Total (1 wicket, 26.3 overs)	156

DNB: MG Bevan, *SR Waugh, DR Martyn, IJ Harvey, SK Warne, B Lee, JN Gillespie, GD McGrath
Fall: 1-78 (ME Waugh)
Bowling: Wasim Akram 7-0-15-0, Waqar Younis 5-0-32-0, Saqlain Mushtaq 8-0-50-0, Abdur Razzaq 5-0-40-0, Azhar Mahmood 1.3-0-18-0

RESULT: AUSTRALIA WON BY NINE WICKETS
UMPIRES: DR SHEPHERD AND P WILLEY
MAN OF THE MATCH: AC GILCHRIST

GAME 30

AUSTRALIA V NEW ZEALAND
VB SERIES
MELBOURNE
29 JANUARY 2002

As I've said a number of times in this book (and a few times quietly to my captains during my career), one of the things I enjoy most in one-day cricket is getting the chance to play a long innings. That was why I wanted to bat at No. 4, and why I was very disappointed when I was dropped back to No. 6 midway through the 2001–02 VB Series. That demotion was one of a number of moves made by the selectors to arrest a sudden dip in form by the Australian team, and while I could understand the logic behind it, that didn't mean I had to agree with it, or enjoy it.

It was a strange experience, the team going through that rough trot. The one-day team had been truly dominant for quite a while, experiencing those winning streaks through 1999–2000, then cruising through the 2000–01 one-day series in Australia against the West Indies and Zimbabwe, winning in India (no mean trick) and dominating in that NatWest series in England. We went into the VB Series having won 45 of our previous 57 one-day internationals (10 losses, two ties), a success rate of 79 per cent. Not bad, four-and-a-half victories for every loss. The Test team had won the Ashes in England and then come back and, after drawing a rain-interrupted series against New Zealand, had thrashed 3–0 in three matches a South African team that was supposed to be the second best Test team in the world.

And then we lost our first three games in the VB Series, not playing particularly well, I'm the first to admit, and the world caved in. According to the media, the rotation system had to go, Steve Waugh couldn't play, Michael Bevan had to be dropped down the order. Sure, we weren't playing well, but I don't think there was too much logic in a lot of what was said and written.

As a No. 6, more often than not you come out to bat with around 10 overs to go, maybe 15, maybe five. When you do pull off an unlikely victory, it is always written up as a great escape, and if you do it a few times, people not only start believing that you can do it all the time, they think that you *have* been doing it all the time. As some of the stories in this book have shown, I have been fortunate enough to get the Australian one-day team out of some tight situations during my career—and that is a part of batting at No. 6 that I enjoy. I've played more than 150 innings in one-day cricket. More often than not, especially when I bat at 6, I'm required to play a small cameo role. My batting average of more than 50 has come about not so much by a succession of big unbeaten scores, but more by a large collection of smaller not outs. I'm not a natural big hitter, so when I come in at No. 6 in the final few overs, inevitably I see my role as getting the ones, hitting the ball into gaps, running as hard as I can.

One of the tricks of trying to win a run chase is to keep your run-rate achievable without taking risks. For this, you need flexibility, calmness and focus on the moment. Having the confidence to seize the opportunity and being able to time your run are the keys in this situation.

Thus I relish the chance to bat for a long time, though I appreciate that when I'm batting No. 6 and such opportunities come about, it means the team is in trouble. Still, from my point of view, these are situations not to be wasted. If I'm in after 10 overs, or 20 overs, whatever, my mind will immediately work out the best way to get my team home, and I'll make my calculations on the basis that we have all the 50 overs available to manufacture the winning runs. I never think in terms of running out of comrades. As far as I'm concerned, my partners will look after me.

In terms of this 2001–02 VB Series, this match at the MCG was something of a do-or-die game for us. After those first three back-to-back losses, we'd recovered somewhat by beating the South Africans twice. We could probably have lost this game against the Kiwis and still made the finals, but it would have been very unlikely, one of those situations in which you need results you can't control to go your way so you can sneak through. Few of our critics appreciated what a good team this New Zealand side was, but we did, and the fact that they came out and batted really well to make 245 was no surprise. We didn't bowl too badly, but Stephen Fleming, Craig McMillan, Chris Cairns and Chris Harris all batted very intelligently. We went into the interval knowing that we'd have to bat well to win, and we thought we would.

But early on in the innings, we didn't. From 0–24 in the fourth over we crashed to 6–82 in the 22nd. I'd come in during the 15th over, at 4–53, which at least gave me plenty of time to build an innings. When Shane Warne came out to join me after Ian Harvey was caught behind off Shane Bond, our task was pretty horrendous: 163 runs to win, four wickets in hand, fractionally less than six runs per over, a run a ball, to get us home.

History records that we managed to achieve that task, and afterwards all the headlines were about my hundred. As much as I tried to deflect the accolades, the focus came back to me, but it is a fact that I was helped enormously by the efforts of the three lower-order guys who batted with me—Shane Warne, Brett Lee and Andy Bichel. They all did fantastic jobs, especially considering the situation and the fact that we had to win. A constant in all my most memorable performances in big-time cricket has been the support of my team-mates. Indeed, in this instance I remember a period—just when it became apparent that we had a genuine winning chance—when I was the one who was getting out of control, and Warney was required to calm me down. Usually when I bat with Shane it's the other way around.

This was one of those match situations in which there needs to be some serious communication between the batsmen out in the middle. Warney and I were continually reminding each other that the plan early on was simply to see out some overs; three or four runs every six balls would do, even until the 30th over. That would get us up to around 6–110, leaving us with another 130 to 140 to get from the last 20, around six-and-a-half to seven runs an over. That, I decided, was manageable. Until the 30-over mark the main objective was to stay calm, don't get out, don't get too far ahead of ourselves. Rotating the strike was important; if we could do that there was no need to panic. We just had to keep doing what we were doing.

We reached the 30-over mark at 6–108, which I imagine most observers, including our opponents, would have thought was too far back for a win. But we were settled in and were ready to up the ante. Interestingly, in the first eight overs Shane and I were together, overs 23 to 30, we scored the following off each over: 2, 2, 2, 4, 4, 4, 3 and 3. For the remainder of the innings, only three times did we score less than five off an over, only once did we go less than four.

From overs 30 to 40, I wanted to keep at around a run a ball. When we got to the end of the 39th over at 7–158 (Warney having been dismissed for 29, from 54 deliveries, three overs earlier, after a 61-run partnership from 92 balls), I realised that, for the first time since Shane and I had come together, we were falling behind the targets that I had set for us. The required run-rate was up to 7.73 runs per over. It was at this point that the game changed. Brett Lee and I took 14 runs from the 40th over, bowled by Chris Harris, including three Bevan boundaries (an on-drive, a square drive and a swing over midwicket), and another 11 from the 41st, bowled by Dion Nash, including two fours by 'Bing'. Thus, with nine overs to go, we needed 63, exactly seven an over. More importantly, the Kiwis now realised that they might not win. Hope builds while fear destroys.

It's a funny thing, but whenever I'm asked about this game, one of the subjects that comes up most is the way the Kiwis handled themselves in the final 10 overs. Always, people refer to the manner in which they suddenly began engaging in a succession of mini-team meetings; every fielder apparently had a theory as to how to stop our advance. Subconsciously, we might have fed off their confusion, their indecisiveness, but the truth is I wasn't really aware of how they were going about their game. It was just one of those times that happen all too rarely. I was 'in the zone', as they say, totally focused on what we were trying to do—win the game.

I was aware of their field placements and the fact that they were constantly changing, because, as I've explained elsewhere, in one-day cricket a bowler *has* to bowl to his field, especially in the final overs. A study of where the fieldsmen are positioned inevitably reveals what sort of line and length the bowler is going to concentrate on. But, with this information locked into my mind-set, I had to make sure that I played every ball on its merits.

In the next four overs we didn't hit a boundary. But we did score at six an over, hitting five twos and 13 singles. So with five overs to go, the assignment was exactly eight an over, 40 runs to win, 30 balls to come. Bing was 21 not out, I was 79. At this point I'd only hit six fours, three of them in that one Chris Harris over. If this innings proved anything, it was that you don't need to hit fours to score at seven or eight an over. You need to turn the strike over, and take the twos. And 'hitting into the gap' can mean more than just bisecting the space between the infielders. If you beat the infield and, in the process, put the ball into the gaps in the outfield, you can get your twos and even threes. On a big ground such as the Melbourne Cricket Ground, with the fieldsmen way back on the fence, a softly-struck stroke through the infield can be two as well, provided you run hard.

Now, though, was the time to go for it, and we took 10 from the 46th over, eight of them mine, including a four and a three. The Melbourne crowd was going berserk, although I wasn't really aware of that until I watched a replay later. I'm sure I fed off their enthusiasm, but I was too preoccupied with winning the game to be fully aware of them. Bing and I continued to talk between nearly every ball, as did the New Zealanders among themselves, constantly tinkering with their fields, which couldn't have helped their bowlers' mind-set. When we took eight from over 47—four singles and two twos—the required run-rate was back down to 7.33, psychologically a huge plus for us. At this point, I was just about sure we would win.

The only thing that could hurt us was a wicket, which unfortunately is what occurred in the 48th over, when Brett lobbed a knee-high full toss to cover. The stand was worth 81 from 66 balls. We hadn't scored a run off either of the first two balls of the over before Bing was dismissed from the third, so a lot had changed awfully quickly. I still felt we could win, but I wasn't certain. Still, the fact we were in with a very big chance was a positive in itself, and, from my point of view, I was feeling very satisfied with myself. Twenty-five overs earlier, my task had been to give us a chance to win, and I had done that. Now, having got so close, I didn't want to throw it away.

In many ways, Andy Bichel was the perfect man to come in at this point. I had been in a similar situation with 'Bic' before, at the Adelaide Oval in late 1997, coincidentally also against New Zealand, when we had come together in the final over with two needed from three balls. Bic came out that day and immediately hit Gavin Larsen for four. I've played against him in domestic limited-overs cricket and he's done the same thing. Boundless energy, nerves of steel, all with a boyish smile—the lad enjoys his cricket.

Here, he came out and blitzed it, scoring a two and three from his first two deliveries and never letting up after that. Meanwhile, after getting a single off the last ball of the 48th over, to retain the strike, I then had a dream time in the 49th over, hitting each of Andre Adams' first five balls for two—to backward point, wide of long off, long off, in front of the sightscreen, and midwicket, respectively. The fourth two got me to my hundred, from 93 balls. Twice in the over the umps called for the video to judge potential run outs at the bowler's end. Twice,

Bic was well in. In these situations, a video call can be a blessing, a chance to get your breath back.

I never faced another ball. After a very lengthy discussion between the New Zealanders, Bic hit the first and third balls of Shane Bond's over for four, backward of point both times, and the game was won. Immediately, I was punching the air and roaring in a manner I rarely do, and the embrace with Bic mid-pitch was as joyous and emotional as any I've experienced in sport. To have your team-mates rush out onto the field to congratulate you in such circumstances is one of the most satisfying of experiences. It was only later, as I dwelt on what we'd done to win the game and, to a degree, restore the team's reputation, that I felt more than a touch of relief as well. It's good to win.

When I hit that last ball of Roger Harper's for four, back on New Year's Day 1996, I had a naïve belief that I was going to wake up the next morning and nothing would have changed. This time, I was ready for the intense celebrity treatment that I knew would last for a day or two. Or at least I thought I was. What I found was that in the six years since the moment that first made my one-day reputation, the status of the Australian team in the Australian community had risen, interest in the side had spread—a product, I imagine, of our success and the aggressive way we play the game. Never was this better captured for me than the next morning, when we arrived at the airport, when I was swamped—no other word for it—by a posse of 20 or 30 reporters and their cameras and microphones. For me, still a shy, introverted sort of bloke, it was off-putting all over again. A day later, and they were on to the next newsflash. But gee it was intense for a while, much more, as I said, than in 1996.

After that, our effort and my hundred would only come up if I was having a quiet drink, or was out to dinner, in the hotel foyer. Then someone would bring the game up, and I'd smile and be only too happy to talk about it.

Any time.

AUSTRALIA V NEW ZEALAND, VB SERIES, 2001–02
MELBOURNE CRICKET GROUND
29 JANUARY 2002 (50-OVERS MATCH)
TOSS: NEW ZEALAND

New Zealand innings

L Vincent c Gilchrist b McGrath	5
NJ Astle c Warne b Lee	11
*SP Fleming run out	50
CD McMillan c Ponting b Harvey	34
CL Cairns c Bevan b Warne	55
CZ Harris run out	41
DJ Nash run out	24
+AC Parore lbw McGrath	1
AR Adams not out	13
DL Vettori not out	0
Extras (lb 4, w 4, nb 3)	11
Total (8 wickets, 50 overs)	245

DNB: SE Bond
Fall: 1-7 (Vincent), 2-19 (Astle), 3-73 (McMillan), 4-143 (Fleming), 5-178 (Cairns), 6-226 (Nash), 7-228 (Parore), 8-235 (Harris)
Bowling: McGrath 10-0-41-2, Lee 8-0-32-1, Bichel 6-0-20-0, Warne 10-0-56-1, Harvey 10-0-59-1, SR Waugh 6-0-33-0

Australia innings

ME Waugh c Adams b Nash	21
+AC Gilchrist b Bond	14
RT Ponting c Astle b Bond	8
DR Martyn c Harris b Adams	6
*SR Waugh c Parore b Nash	7
MG Bevan not out	102
IJ Harvey c Parore b Bond	12
SK Warne c Bond b Adams	29
B Lee c Astle b Bond	27
AJ Bichel not out	13
Extras (w 3, nb 6)	9
Total (8 wickets, 49.3 overs)	248

DNB: GD McGrath
Fall: 1-24 (Gilchrist), 2-40 (Ponting), 3-51 (ME Waugh), 4-53 (Martyn), 5-65 (SR Waugh), 6-82 (Harvey), 7-143 (Warne), 8-224 (Lee)
Bowling: Nash 9-0-50-2, Bond 9.3-2-38-4, Adams 10-0-52-2, Vettori 10-0-36-0, Harris 8-0-50-0, Astle 3-0-22-0

RESULT: AUSTRALIA WON BY TWO WICKETS
UMPIRES: DB HAIR AND SJA TAUFEL
MAN OF THE MATCH: MG BEVAN